Mastering Financial
Markets with Python

Mastering Financial Markets with Python

New Horizons in Technical Analysis

Sofien Kaabar, CFA

BEP

BUSINESS EXPERT PRESS

Leader in applied, concise business books

Mastering Financial Markets with Python:
New Horizons in Technical Analysis

First published in 2026 by
Business Expert Press, LLC
222 East 46th Street, New York, NY 10017
www.businessexpertpress.com

ISBN-13: 978-1-63742-926-6 (paperback)
ISBN-13: 978-1-63742-927-3 (e-book)

Finance and Financial Management Collection

First edition: 2026

10 9 8 7 6 5 4 3 2 1

EU SAFETY REPRESENTATIVE
Mare Nostrum Group B.V.
Mauritskade 21D
1091 GC Amsterdam
The Netherlands
gpsr@mare-nostrum.co.uk

Description

Master Technical Analysis in the Age of Python and Innovation.

Financial markets are evolving, and so should your strategies. *Mastering Financial Markets with Python: New Horizons in Technical Analysis* bridges the gap between traditional methods and the new era of data-driven analysis. This book equips you with the skills to design, implement, and evaluate advanced technical analysis techniques all through a practical, code-first approach.

Inside, you will learn how to do the following:

- Rethink and modernize classic indicators with Python.
- Build advanced volatility and moving average indicators.
- Detect and analyze harmonic and reversal patterns automatically.
- Detect and analyze timing patterns automatically.
- Apply enhanced Fibonacci techniques and alternative charting systems.
- Develop a new generation of technical indicators tailored to modern markets.

This book provides hands-on tools to master today's fast-paced financial landscape. By combining innovation with Python, you'll gain a deeper understanding of markets and build smarter, more adaptive strategies.

Why buy it now? Because trading edges are fleeting, and those who master Python-driven technical analysis will be the ones shaping the markets of tomorrow.

Contents

List of Figures

Introduction

Technical analysis plays a complex function in the world of financial markets, as traders are always looking for more accurate and reliable ways to interpret market behavior. For many years, traditional technical analysis has been a dependable toolkit due to its reliance on chart patterns and well-known indicators like Bollinger bands and moving averages. However, the emergence of a new age in technical analysis—one that embraces the potential of sophisticated algorithms and overcomes the constraints of classical techniques—has been made possible by the introduction of modern computing power and the accessibility of large amounts of data. The book is intended for aspiring and professional traders who want to use the power of technology to obtain a competitive advantage in the markets, as well as coders who want to add more tools to their arsenal. Python, a strong and flexible programming language that has established itself as the industry standard for many market activities, is at the center of this change. You can move beyond static analysis and toward dynamic, data-driven insights that can adapt to ever-changing market conditions. **Chapter 1** introduces everything you need to know to understand technical analysis and its applications to time series. In addition to being exposed to technical tools, you will end the chapter with an introduction to modern technical analysis and its objectives. **Chapter 2** gets you up to speed with your Python skills in order to understand what's to come later. Topics, such as basic syntax, functions, control flow, and data import, are covered extensively in a straightforward manner. **Chapter 3** explores modern approaches to technical analysis, presenting innovative ways to utilize classic indicators like the relative strength index (RSI) and Bollinger bands beyond traditional methods. It also introduces entirely new indicators derived from the combination of existing ones, with the goal of enhancing market analysis and providing fresh insights into price behavior. **Chapter 4** introduces innovative charting mechanisms, including Heikin-Ashi, K's candlesticks, and volume candlesticks. The primary objective is to broaden your perspective on time series analysis, offering alternative visual interpretations of price action that may reveal underlying market dynamics often overlooked by conventional methods. **Chapter 5** enters the world of Fibonacci techniques for trading, emphasizing Python's role in uncovering lesser-known Fibonacci assumptions. You will get to code Fibonacci techniques such as the 23.6% reintegration. **Chapter 6** delves into the realm of volatility indicators, offering tools to better interpret the fluctuations in price action. A variety of indicators are introduced, each accompanied by clear explanations of the underlying intuition, equipping you with a deeper understanding of market dynamics and volatility behavior. Building on the foundation of classic candlestick patterns, **Chapter 7** introduces modern variations that enhance the ability to interpret price action. These patterns serve as powerful tools for understanding market behavior in modern trading environments. **Chapter 8** delves into the fascinating world of harmonic patterns, explaining their structure and relevance in market analysis. It includes step-by-step guidance on coding these patterns in Python, enabling you to evaluate their efficacy. **Chapter 9** focuses on timing patterns, an innovative approach that integrates price and time to generate top and bottom market signals. You will gain insights into the interplay between temporal and price-based market dynamics. **Chapter 10** revisits timeless price patterns, such as double tops and double bottoms, through the lens of Python programming. You will learn how to code these patterns and evaluate their profitability. Serving as the core of this book, **Chapter 11** unveils my personal collection of indicators. Each indicator is presented in detail, including its intuition, coding, and application. This chapter is packed with insights and advanced techniques. **Chapter 12** offers a comprehensive guide to evaluating trading strategies through essential concepts in performance evaluation, back-testing, and risk management. You will gain hands-on experience coding performance metrics, empowering you to assess and refine your trading approaches with confidence. By the end of this book, you will have a comprehensive understanding of how to take advantage of Python to enhance your technical analysis capabilities. This book will serve as a valuable resource on your journey to mastering new horizons of technical analysis.

CHAPTER 1

Classic Technical Analysis Versus Modern Technical Analysis

Technical analysis is the study of charts with the aim of inferring the next market direction given historical results and hypotheses. Therefore, you try to forecast the market based on past patterns and price action with the aid of technical indicators. Within the large field of technical analysis, there are many diverse types of tools, such as the following:

- Price action and trend analysis: Charts are visual representations of time series on which you apply techniques that help the forecasting process. To locate inflection levels and predict the next move, techniques like drawing trend lines and pivot points are often used.
- Indicator analysis: In this type of analysis, mathematical formulae are used to develop objective indicators that can either be trend following or contrarian. Moving averages and the RSI, two well-known indicators, are covered in further detail in this chapter.
- Pattern recognition: A pattern is typically an event that occasionally occurs with a specific expected outcome based on empirical observations. Patterns can come in various forms, such as gaps, candlestick configurations, and price patterns. You will develop a deep knowledge of pattern recognition as you progress through the book.

Technical analysis relies primarily on three different assumptions. The first one is that history repeats itself. Clusters are frequently visible throughout trends and ranges. Some specific configurations and patterns are likely to produce results that are comparable (but never guaranteed). This presupposes a nonrandom probability with predictable properties over the long term. The fact is: history most likely rhymes rather than repeats itself.[1] The second assumption is that the market discounts everything, meaning all fundamental, technical, and quantitative information is presumed to be contained in the current price. And lastly, the third assumption is that market movement occurs in waves. This means that trading occurs at varied frequencies because of different time frames, which leads to patterns and waves instead of a straight line. Technical analysis also assumes that markets are not efficient, but what does that imply? According to the efficient market hypothesis (EMH), price and value are the same thing, and information is already included in the current price (thus reflecting perfectly the asset's value). When you purchase an asset, you expect it to be undervalued (in the lingo of fundamental analysis) or oversold (in the lingo of technical analysis), and for that reason, you think the price will rise to match the value. As a result, you're assuming that the value is greater than the price the moment you buy it. The EMH suggests that any active trading must not produce above-average returns because it refutes any assertions that the price does not equal the value of an asset. Active trading is the act of engaging in speculative operations to outperform a certain benchmark, which is typically an index or a weighted measure. The EMH is the greatest nemesis of technical analysis since one of its first tenets is that technical analysis cannot provide excess profits under weak forms of efficiency. As a result, technical analysis is disproved from the start, and fundamental analysis follows suit with a similar hammering. Given the volume of market participants and the ease of access to information, it is reasonable to assume that markets may eventually become perfectly efficient in the future. However, human interventions and other exogenous factors may still cause market anomalies that can be exploited.

Charts can be composed of lines or scatter points, but the ones of interest are candlestick charts. To understand candlestick charts, you must

---

[1] A quote generally attributed to Mark Twain and Theodor Reik.

understand the concept of candlesticks. Consider the following chrono-logical information of a certain financial instrument:

- The market opens at $1.00.
- The market shapes a high of $1.04 and a low of $0.98 during trading.
- The market finally closes at $1.02.

These four pieces of information are the building blocks of financial time series, and they are referred to as OHLC data (open, high, low, and close). Candlesticks are box-shaped OHLC representations for every time step (e.g., hourly or daily). The following theoretical illustration shows the candlestick of the previous example (Figure 1.1).

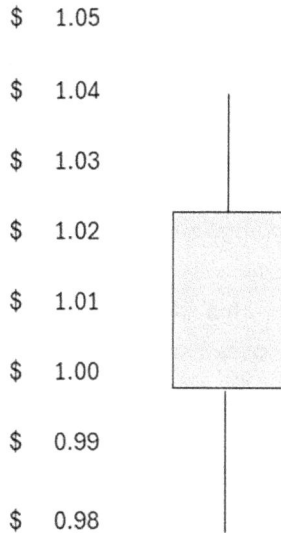

$ 1.05

$ 1.04

$ 1.03

$ 1.02

$ 1.01

$ 1.00

$ 0.99

$ 0.98

Figure 1.1 A bullish candlestick

Now consider the following OHLC values:

- The market opens at $1.00.
- The market shapes a high of $1.02 and a low of $0.98 during trading.
- The market finally closes at $0.99 (Figure 1.2).

$ 1.05

$ 1.04

$ 1.03

$ 1.02

$ 1.01

$ 1.00

$ 0.99

$ 0.98

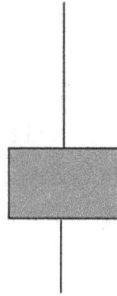

Figure 1.2 A bearish candlestick

Time series refers to a sequence of data points collected, recorded, or measured at successive points in time. In simpler terms, it's like a set of observations or measurements taken over a period of time, where each data point is associated with a specific moment or interval. Time series can come from various sources and can represent different phenomena, such as market prices, weather patterns, economic indicators, or any other measurable quantity that changes over time. A regime is the present and past directional state of the market. There are three main regimes:

- A bullish market where the general trend is ascending
- A bearish market where the general trend is descending
- A ranging market where the general trend is sideways

Let's start with the first technical tool, price action and trend analysis. Analyzing charts using price action entails using visual interpretations of the past reactions around certain levels or certain alignments. The first technique is to draw horizontal support/resistance lines or to draw ascending/descending trend lines (Figure 1.3).

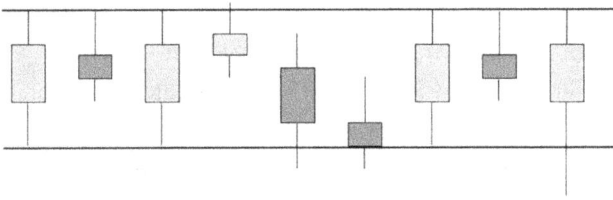

Figure 1.3 A ranging/sideways configuration

The intuition behind horizontal support and resistance lines comes from the basic principles of supply and demand, as well as psychology in trading. A support level is a price point where an asset tends to stop falling and start rising again. It's essentially a floor that the price struggles to break below. Think of it like the price of an asset encountering a soft spot where buyers are willing to step in and purchase, preventing the price from falling further. At this level, demand (buying pressure) is strong enough to offset selling pressure. Over time, when the price of an asset falls to a certain level and then bounces back up multiple times, traders begin to recognize that level as a point where the asset tends to find support. A resistance level is a price point where an asset tends to stop rising and starts to fall back down. It's like a ceiling for the price. This is a price point where selling pressure overcomes buying pressure. Sellers come in at this level, expecting the price to drop, which causes the price to fall back down. Similar to support, resistance forms when the price hits a level multiple times and is unable to break above it. Traders recognize this price point as a ceiling and often sell when the price approaches it. Support and resistance lines don't have to be horizontal; they can also have a trending nature in them as illustrated by Figure 1.4.

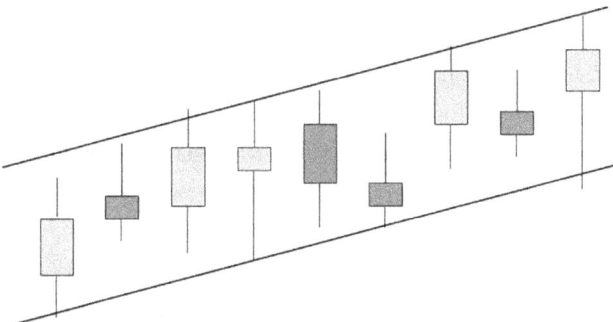

Figure 1.4 A trending configuration

The more frequently a price hits a specific level (either resistance or support), the more traders begin to expect it to serve as a barrier. A self-fulfilling prophecy is produced by this repeated interaction. When the price approaches again, market participants are more likely to respond to these important levels because they recall them from the past. If the price breaks above a resistance level, it suggests that demand is strong enough to push the price higher, turning the resistance into a potential support level. Similarly, if a price falls below support, the former support might turn into resistance. Sometimes, round levels (also known as psychological levels) play a crucial role in trading, often acting as natural support and resistance levels where price action tends to react. These clean levels, such as 100 or 200 on currency pairs like USDJPY and EURJPY, are popular among traders because they are simple to remember and frequently used. When buying or selling interest clusters, they may thus turn into self-fulfilling barriers. In the case of EURNZD, for instance, the price has historically struggled to break above the 2.0000 level, which has served as a significant resistance zone in 2020 and 2025. These levels are useful benchmarks for entries, exits, and risk management since traders frequently expect a reversal or breakout when the price gets close to such a round number. In conclusion, the support and resistance lines are shaped in part by the collective behavior, experience, and expectation of traders regarding these levels. Indicator analysis comes next.

Indicator Analysis

This book presents many new and old indicators that you will be able to fully understand and use. We can start with the two best-known indicators, moving averages and the RSI. Moving averages are, without a doubt, the number one technical tool used by all types of traders, strategists, and analysts. They allow you to have a view of the current trend and to also have a dynamic (moving) support/resistance line. Moving averages are associated with simple and complex trading strategies and can be a component of many different trading techniques. When you have a set of observations and you want to describe the data, you generally use the mean as a representative (in case there are not a huge number of outliers). The mean is also used as the next expected value in the case of a chronologically listed dataset (this is also considered the simplest prediction technique). To calculate the mean of a dataset, divide the sum by the quantity. Look at the following table populated by chronological variables:

t	$t + 1$	$t + 2$	$t + 3$	$t + 4$
10	12	11	12	14

The first row refers to time. The second row refers to the values of the variables. If you keep in mind the intuition of the mean (the sum by the quantity), you will formulate the following:

$$\text{Mean} = \frac{10 + 12 + 11 + 12 + 14}{5} = 11.80$$

Therefore, the mean of the dataset is 11.80 (thus, a moving average with a lookback of five periods will have a value of 11.80 at $t+4$). A moving average is a mean that moves on a rolling basis using a predetermined lookback period (quantity). If you want to create a 5-period moving average, then you will take a dataset and at each time step, you will calculate the mean of the last five values (including the current one). Then, you will drop the first one and include the new value in the new time step. This is why it is referred to as a moving average. Figure 1.5 shows a 5-period moving average on a candlestick chart.

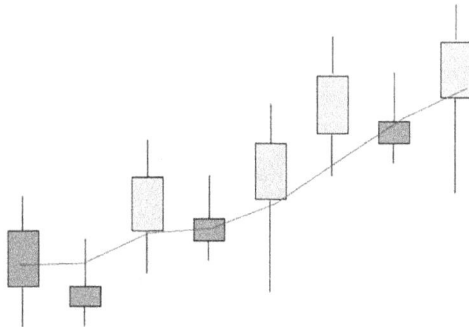

Figure 1.5 A 5-period simple moving average

Moving averages are primarily used for trend identification. A rising moving average suggests an uptrend, while a falling moving average indicates a downtrend. Additionally, moving averages often act as dynamic support and resistance. In an uptrend, the price may bounce off the moving average as support. In a downtrend, the moving average may act as resistance.

The next indicator is the RSI (which stands for relative strength index). Also known as the father of all indicators, the RSI is the go-to tool for most technical analysts, traders, and investors. This is why it's important that you master it. Developed by J. Welles Wilder Jr. in the 70s and introduced in his book *New Concepts in Technical Trading*, the RSI is an oscillator calculated purely from the close price and is bound between 0 and 100. It measures the speed and change of price movements and is primarily used to find overbought and oversold conditions. But first, let's see how to calculate the RSI. The first step is to determine the price change for each period within the chosen time frame (typically 14 periods). The price change (delta) for each period is calculated by subtracting the previous closing price from the current closing price:

$$\Delta_i = \text{Close}_i - \text{Close}_{i-1}$$

If the result is positive, it's a gain. If the result is negative, take its absolute value and consider it a loss (therefore, separating the two and keeping two columns representing gains and absolute losses). Once you have the price changes for each period, the next step is to calculate the average gain and absolute average loss over the specified period (14 periods in this example). The initial average gain and average loss are calculated as follows:

$$\text{Average gain}_0 = \frac{\text{Sum of gains over 14 periods}}{14}$$
$$\text{Average loss}_0 = \frac{\text{Sum of losses over 14 periods}}{14}$$

After calculating the initial average gain and loss, the subsequent average gain and loss are smoothed using the following formula:

$$\text{Average gain}_i = \frac{(\text{Average gain}_{i-1} \times 13) + \text{gain}_i}{14}$$
$$\text{Average loss}_i = \frac{(\text{Average loss}_{i-1} \times 13) + \text{loss}_i}{14}$$

The relative strength (RS) is calculated by dividing the average gain by the average loss:

$$RS_i = \frac{\text{Average gain}_i}{\text{Average loss}_i}$$

Finally, the RSI is calculated using the RS value in the RSI formula:

$$RSI_i = 100 - \frac{100}{1 + RS_i}$$

As new data comes in, the RSI is recalculated with the new closing prices, continuously updating to reflect the latest market conditions. The smoothing process ensures that the RSI reacts to recent price changes but is also influenced by the past 14 periods, providing a balanced view of momentum. Figure 1.6 shows hypothetical RSI values.

As the RSI's values are naturally and mathematically bounded between 0 and 100, values close to the lower end (~30) are correlated with imminent phases of recovery, while values close to the upper end (~70) are correlated with imminent phases of correction. This correlation does not imply causation, which means that in many instances, if the RSI is close to 30, it does not guarantee any recovery. Additionally, it is not a timing indicator, and thus, the recovery may come with a delay, which can disturb the trading process. In any case, the RSI must only be used as a confirmation tool to help raise your conviction of a preexisting directional bias. It's interesting to know that the correlation between changes in the RSI and changes in the market is near perfect. Now, we will discuss modern technical analysis, the protagonist of this book, which harbors the principles and foundations of the subsequent chapters.

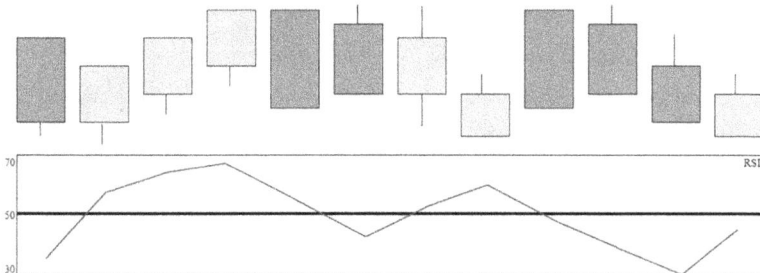

Figure 1.6 A theoretical illustration of the RSI

Modern Technical Analysis

Modern technical analysis is a selection of techniques, hypotheses, enhancements, and new indicators by which I aim to address the weaknesses of classic technical analysis. First, we need to understand the said weaknesses of classic technical analysis:

- The subjectivity of signals and directional views: Psychology is one of the pillars of technical analysis, and with that, a great deal of subjectivity comes into place. Many patterns, signals, and techniques are mostly left to the discretion of analysts and traders. This means that a sizable portion of classic technical analysis lacks an objective rules-based framework that determines what works and what does not. You will see such examples in the coming chapters.

- The back-testing challenges: Some classic techniques are so subjective that it may be impossible to back-test them without altering a major part of them. For example, veteran technical analysts may use Elliot wave theory[2] to decompose the markets; however, this technique is extremely subjective and relies on the discretion of the user. Graphical support and resistance lines are also hard to back-test since each analyst may choose to draw them differently.

- The fitting paradox: Some techniques suffer from a fitting problem. For example, Elliot wave theory forces the market to always be in a certain wave count. This means that a great deal of hindsight is in play when looking at the past. Additionally, some patterns may seem obvious when looked at after they have unfolded, contrary to when they are forming. Hindsight bias is a major issue in the world of trading and analysis.

- The rusty indicators issue: After decades of applying the same indicators with the same parameters on ever-evolving markets, it

---

[2]Elliott wave theory is a technical analysis framework that suggests market prices move in predictable patterns called waves. These waves are divided into five impulsive waves in the direction of the trend, followed by three corrective waves against it. The theory is based on the belief that market psychology drives price action in repetitive cycles.

may be time to update them, as many are failing to capture the transforming statistical and chaotic nature of current-day time series. Trading 40 to 50 years ago involved less use of machines and modern pattern recognition techniques, which resulted in different market dynamics. Historically, classic technical indicators worked well, but as markets evolve and adapt, indicators may start losing their efficacy.

- The self-fulfilling prophecy: When a number of traders see the same pattern, they will likely act on it and actually validate it. This makes the pattern work for the wrong reasons. The dangerous part of this event is that it invalidates the initial hypothesis and turns the forecast/trade into plain luck.
- The reliance on a few technical indicators with high intraclass correlation: Many classic technical indicators are extremely correlated to one another, and do not offer much in terms of diversification. For example, the RSI's signal is likely to be seen at the same time on other technical indicators. Throughout the book, you will be exposed to a number of modern indicators. Modern technical indicators have a relatively low correlation with each other, offering a better diversification factor.

Modern technical analysis tries to address the issues mentioned in the previous list. Let's see how:

- Modern technical analysis addresses the subjectivity of signals by always having clear and rules-based signals. There is no subjective interpretations in modern technical analysis.
- Modern technical analysis addresses the back-testing challenges the same way it does for the first point. Strict conditions and rules are related to an easier back-testing framework. Performance evaluation metrics will be discussed in Chapter 12.
- Modern technical analysis addresses the fitting paradox by simply eliminating any classic techniques that assume any type of fitting. For example, Elliot wave theory in its classic form is not valid in modern technical analysis. However, it can be rendered objective through the use of smart algorithms.

- Modern technical analysis addresses the rusty indicators problem by offering a myriad of new indicators with different calculation methods that try to take into account the ever-evolving market dynamics. Indicators like K's reversal indicator II take into account the price, time, and moving averages in order to find directional signals. This three-dimensional characteristic decorrelates the signals from other indicators, and thus adds further conviction.
- Modern technical analysis addresses the self-fulfilling prophecy issue simply by the fact that modern indicators are unknown and are therefore unlikely to suffer from this issue.
- Modern technical analysis addresses the high intraclass correlation problem by presenting uncorrelated indicators with different calculation methods, making the use of two or more modern indicators theoretically more useful than using two or more classic indicators. Modern technical analysis considers the marginal increase in predictability with the addition of indicators and techniques to the framework. The condition for this is for the indicator to have a better-than-random forecasting ability. In other words, it behooves the predictability to have two uncorrelated indicators with accuracy greater than 50%. In contrast, there is no added value from having two extremely correlated indicators with accuracy greater than 50%.

Additionally, modern technical analysis considers that every market has varying regimes and statistical properties. This means that strategies and indicators can have golden eras where their predictive power is high, but can also have bad eras where they underperform, due to the nature of their signals. Modern technical analysis suggests the following solution to such issues:

- For reversal and trend-following indicators: Bullish signals within an ascending trend have more weight than bearish signals within an ascending trend. Additionally, bearish signals in a descending trend have more weight than bearish signals in a descending trend.
- During sideways regimes, both bullish signals and bearish signals have the same weight.

Modern technical analysis also bridges the gap between other types of analysis by incorporating sentiment and quantitative techniques into the overall trading/investing framework. For example:

- Sentiment analysis incorporation: An example of this would be to apply a modern technical indicator on a sentiment indicator, such as the put-call ratio.[3]
- Quantitative analysis incorporation: An example of this would be to run a machine learning algorithm on a technical indicator in order to predict the underlying's values.

Modern technical analysis contains the following tools:

- Modern indicators: These can be raw indicators built entirely from scratch or structured indicators, which are a fusion between different indicators.
- Modern patterns: These can be candlestick patterns that are not present in the classic literature of technical analysis (e.g., the double trouble pattern) or timing patterns (e.g., the Fibonacci timing pattern).
- Modern techniques: These are new ways to use classic indicators. Instead of using the RSI as recommended by the original creator, I recommend exploring new techniques that aim to improve the signals and target the weaknesses of classic techniques. An example of a modern technique is the V technique on the RSI.

This chapter provided a brief overview of two distinct approaches to analyzing financial markets, classic technical analysis and modern technical analysis, which is a more advanced complement (or alternative if you are a skeptic of classic technical analysis). We explored the foundational principles of technical analysis, including charting techniques

---

[3]The put-call ratio is a sentiment indicator that compares the trading volume of put options to call options. A high ratio suggests bearish sentiment (more puts being traded), while a low ratio indicates bullish sentiment (more calls being traded). It helps gauge market expectations and potential reversals.

and indicators. However, as markets have become more complex and data-driven, the chapter highlighted the limitations of technical analysis, introducing modern analysis techniques as a solution. In the next chapter, you will see how to use Python with time series. By integrating Python into your workflow, you will explore how to apply computational techniques to improve decision making and predictions in financial markets using more advanced technical analysis tools.

CHAPTER 2

Exploring Time Series Analysis with Python

Coding is no longer exclusive to experts nowadays and is rapidly becoming an essential skill. Furthermore, financial coding helps you speed up your analyses, back-tests, and any interpretation that may otherwise take you too much time to do manually. This chapter serves as a refresher to your Python skills, but also shows how to import and visualize historical data, which is paramount to the analyses. Your learning outcome from this chapter is to be able to have a basic understanding of the code, as well as being comfortable with the different data importing and visualization functions. A dedicated GitHub repository is freely accessible at this link.[4] It contains all the code required to run the algorithms of this book.

Downloading Python

Software used to write and run code using Python syntax is called an interpreter. I make use of Spyder. The procedure is the same, even though some people might be more experienced with other interpreters. Spyder can be downloaded from the official website, although downloading it as part of Anaconda, a larger package that gives more features and simplifies installation, is preferable. Keep in mind that Spyder is free to use and open source. Python code is stored in files identified by the .py extension. It is possible to navigate between and open numerous code files when using the interpreter.

Spyder provides an interface with a combination of tools that makes programming easier. Figure 2.1 shows the Spyder window in detail.

---

[4]GitHub repository link: https://github.com/sofienkaabar/mastering-financial -markets-in-python

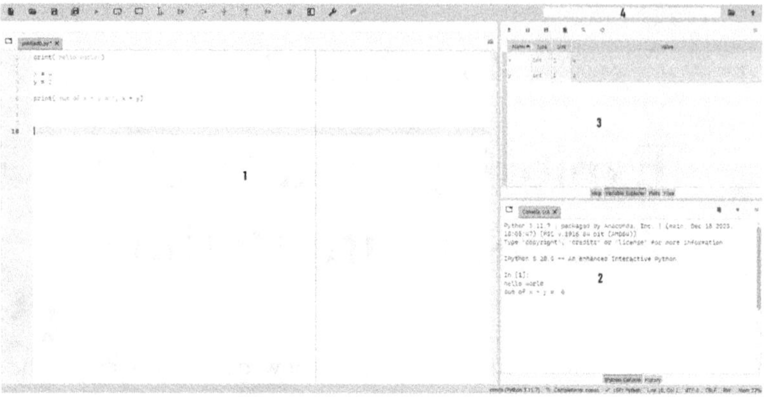

Figure 2.1 Spyder's interface

Let's discover Spyder's main elements:

1. The editor is where you write your Python scripts. It supports syntax highlighting and code completion. Multiple files can be opened simultaneously in different tabs.
2. The console is where you will find the output of your code. This can range from results and errors to even plots.
3. The variable explorer shows the variables you have created in the current session. You can inspect variables, arrays, and data frames from here, making it useful for debugging. Double-clicking a variable opens a data frame or array in a spreadsheet-style viewer.
4. The file explorer lets you browse files and directories on your system. You can quickly open Python files or other documents from here. This is where the current directory lies. You can change it accordingly (e.g., if you need Python to access a file in a certain path).

Additionally, the help pane gives you detailed documentation about functions, libraries, and classes that you're using. If you hover over a function in the editor and press Ctrl + I, the documentation will appear in the help pane. Most of the work done will occur in the editor and the variable explorer. Spyder, bundled with Anaconda, is an ideal starting point for Python programming. Its intuitive interface lowers the barrier to entry, allowing you to focus on logic and problem-solving, not technical setup. You will now see a basic Python introductory course with key elements to focus on in order to be able to write and debug your own code. Keep in mind that it's not a full Python course; therefore, you may need to seek external help for more advanced programming.

Basic Syntax and Operators

The set of guidelines known as syntax specifies the arrangement of statements required to construct functional code. It's crucial to ensure that a computer understands you when you communicate with it. Code can be categorized into executable and nonexecutable code. Executable code forms the majority and is the part that will deliver an output. Nonexecutable code (comments) is used to provide context for the executable code that follows. To help other programmers understand the code, comments are utilized. Python comments start with the hash symbol (#):

```
# This is a comment. It will not be executed by the interpreter
```

The simplest statement in Python is the **print** statement, which returns the values inside the parentheses:

```
print("Hello world!") # this statement will return Hello world! as an output
```

The majority of programming tasks start with arithmetic operations. They enable us to carry out both simple and complex mathematical computations. Arithmetic operators in Python are keywords or symbols that carry out operations on numbers, including subtraction, addition, and more. Mathematical operations between two operands (numbers or variables) are carried out using arithmetic operators. Numerous operators that work with integers, floating-point numbers, and even complex numbers are supported by Python.

Operator	Symbol	Description	Example
Addition	+	Adds two numbers.	$5 + 3 = 8$
Subtraction	−	Subtracts one number from another.	$5 − 3 = 2$
Multiplication	×	Multiplies two numbers.	$5 × 3 = 15$
Division	/	Divides one number by another (returns a float).	$5 / 2 = 2.5$
Floor division	//	Divides and returns the largest whole number (integer).	$5 // 2 = 2$
Modulus	%	Returns the remainder of division.	$5 \% 2 = 1$
Exponentiation	**	Raises a number to the power of another.	$2 ** 3 = 8$

Variables and Data Structures

Python's fundamental ideas of variables and data structures let you store, manage, and work with data. Data frames are a fundamental component of data analysis since they are essential for managing structured, tabular data. A named storage location for data is called a variable. Variables in Python are dynamic, which means that their type is decided at runtime and subject to change. Use the following syntax to define a variable.

```
age = 25              # defining an integer
name = "Alice"        # strings must be between quotation marks
height = 5.7          # a float is a number that contains decimals
is_student = True     # boolean operators take two arguments: True or False
```

Variables must start with a letter or an underscore and cannot contain special characters or spaces. They are also case sensitive. The following code creates two variables, **age** and **Age**, and then compares their value using a Boolean operator (which returns **True** if the statement is true and returns **False** if the statement is false).

```
age = 25
Age = 30
Age == age # returns false when comparing the two different variables
```

The distinction between the single equals sign **=** and the double equals sign **==** is one of the most frequent sources of confusion for novice

Python users. Despite their similar appearance, they have quite different functions:

- The single equals sign `=` is used to assign a value to a variable.
- The double equals sign `==` is used to check whether two values are equal. It doesn't assign anything—it asks a question and returns `True` or `False`.

Data is efficiently arranged and stored using a data structure. Python comes with a number of built-in data structures, including dictionaries, sets, tuples, and lists. For advanced data handling, data frames from the `pandas` library are widely used and will be used in this book. A data frame is a two-dimensional, tabular data structure. Think of it as a spreadsheet or a SQL table in Python. Data frames are highly versatile and are used extensively in data analysis and manipulation. Data frames can be created from various data sources, such as lists, dictionaries, `numpy` arrays, or external files. Figure 2.2 shows a data frame in Spyder.

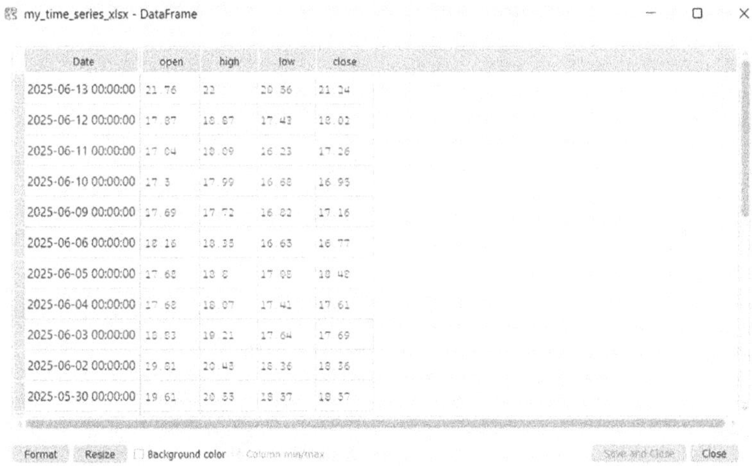

Date	open	high	low	close
2025-06-13 00:00:00	21.76	22	20.36	21.24
2025-06-12 00:00:00	17.87	18.87	17.43	18.02
2025-06-11 00:00:00	17.04	18.09	16.23	17.26
2025-06-10 00:00:00	17.3	17.99	16.68	16.95
2025-06-09 00:00:00	17.69	17.72	16.82	17.16
2025-06-06 00:00:00	18.16	18.35	16.63	16.77
2025-06-05 00:00:00	17.68	18.8	17.08	18.48
2025-06-04 00:00:00	17.68	18.07	17.41	17.61
2025-06-03 00:00:00	18.83	19.21	17.64	17.69
2025-06-02 00:00:00	19.81	20.43	18.36	18.36
2025-05-30 00:00:00	19.61	20.53	18.37	18.57

Figure 2.2 A data frame

You can either generate a data frame in Python using random variables or import one from external parties (e.g., online databases and locally hosted spreadsheets). Use the following code to import data frames from files already on your computer.

```
my_data_frame = pd.read_csv("data.csv")      # to import a csv from a local spreadsheet file
my_data_frame = pd.read_excel("data.xlsx")   # to import an xlsx file from a local spreadsheet file
```

It's important that before importing a data frame from a certain location, you make sure that it shares the same path as Spyder's directory. For example, if your file is on your Desktop, Spyder's directory, as shown as number 4 in Figure 2.1, must also be located on the Desktop. Data frames have named columns, which render them accessible using Python commands. For example, if you only want to access the close price in a multicolumn data frame, you just need to specify it.

```
my_data_frame ["close"]              # access a single column named close
my_data_frame [["high", "low"]]      # access the high and low columns
```

To create a new empty column within an already existing data frame called **my_data_frame**, use the following syntax.

```
my_data_frame ["new_column"] = []        # create a new empty column called new_column
```

Accessing different rows and columns is crucial in manipulating data frames.

```
my_data_frame.iloc[0]          # access the first row
my_data_frame.iloc[-1]         # access the last row
my_data_frame.iloc[0:3]        # access the first three rows (starting with row 0 until row 2)
my_data_frame.iloc[:, 0]       # access the first column
my_data_frame.iloc[:, -1]      # access the last column
my_data_frame.iloc[0, 1]       # access the cell located at the first row of the second column
my_data_frame.loc[0, "close"]  # access the first three rows (starting with row 0 until row 2)
```

You may notice that the last line of the previous code uses **loc** as opposed to **iloc**. The latter accesses data by index label. It's used when you know row/column labels, while the former accesses data by index position. It's used when you know row/column positions. You can also filter your data frames using specific conditions.

```
filtered_data = my_data_frame[my_data_frame["close"] > 30] # create a new data frame with conditions
```

If instead you want to add the filters to the same data frame as opposed to creating a new data frame called **filtered_data**, use the following code.

```
my_data_frame["new_column"] = my_data_frame["close"] > 30 # create a column with conditions
```

When you need to calculate rolling values on your data frame (e.g., a 5-period rolling moving average of the close price), you can use the following code.

```
my_data_frame["moving_average"] = my_data_frame["close"].rolling(window=5).mean()
```

To calculate the rolling 5-period standard deviation, use the following code.

```
my_data_frame["standard_deviation"] = my_data_frame["close"].rolling(window=5).std()
```

Rest assured that you will fully understand the concept of moving averages and standard deviation in detail in the coming chapters.

Control Flow

In Python, control flow describes the sequence in which specific instructions, statements, or function calls are carried out or assessed. It enables decision making, action repetition, and conditional code execution by your program in response to logical rules or conditions. Consider the following sample of code.

```
stock_price = 100
if stock_price < 100:
  print("Price has dropped.")
elif stock_price == 100:
  print("Price has remained the same")
else:
  print("Price has gone up.")
```

As such, if is used at the beginning of conditional sentences. After that, elif—a combination of else and if—is used for each additional, distinct condition until the else statement—which uses the remainder of the probability universe as a condition on its own—makes sense. Because the else statement exists to cover the remainder of the unexplored universe, it does not require a condition. Let's switch to loops now. Code blocks are continually run inside loops until a predetermined condition is satisfied.

When working with time series, loops are occasionally used to compute indicators. The **for** statement is the main looping protagonist and is used to iterate over a finite and specified sequence or a range of elements (e.g., the length of a data frame). For instance, the code that follows uses a loop to compute a compounded savings fund with an interest rate of 5%:

```
savings = 0
annual_contribution = 1000
interest_rate = 0.05
for year in range(1, 6):
# 5 years as Python doesn't take into account the last value in a loop
  savings += annual_contribution
  savings *= (1 + interest_rate)
  print(f"Year {year}: ${savings:.2f}")
```

It can be useful to have two additional statements inside loops. The continue statement moves straight to the following loop iteration, bypassing the remainder of the current loop iteration. Regardless of the loop's condition or number of iterations, the break statement instantly ends the loop in which it is inserted. Here's a basic illustration.

```
stock_prices = [105, 102, 99, 95, 92, 89, 91, 88, 86, 120]
for price in stock_prices:
  if price > 100:
   continue # skip expensive stocks
  print(f"Checking price: ${price}")
  elif price < 90:
   print(f"Buy signal at ${price}!")
  break # stop once we find a good buying  opportunity
```

The **continue** statement skips prices over $100 as we only want to check cheaper stocks. When the algorithm finds a price below $90, it prints a buy signal and uses **break** to stop the loop—assuming we only want the first good deal. Mastering control flow enables you to write smarter, more flexible, and more efficient programs. It's the foundation for building logic-driven applications.

Functions

Functions are reusable code segments that, when called, carry out particular operations. By dividing complicated programs into smaller, more manageable components, they enable developers to write code that is cleaner, more modular, and easier to maintain. Python programming relies heavily on functions, which can be either built-in or user-defined. For instance, len() is a built-in function that returns the length of a data structure. The **def** keyword, the function's name, and parentheses are used to define a function in Python. Here's an illustration.

```
def candlestick_range(high, low):
  return high - low
```

The function in this example, called **candlestick_range**, returns (outputs) the difference between the user-inputted high price and low price. Parentheses are used to pass parameters, which are inputs that functions can accept. Functions can process data dynamically thanks to parameters.

```
candlestick_range(100, 60) # the output will be 40
```

The **return** keyword allows a function to return a value. When a function reaches a return statement, it exits the function and returns a result to the caller. It's critical to realize that variables defined inside a function are only accessible within that function due to their local scope. With functions, you can write code once and use it repeatedly without creating duplicates. Compared to a large, monolithic block of code, smaller, modular functions are simpler to debug, update, and maintain. Functions encourage abstraction by allowing you to use them without having to comprehend all of their finer points. Throughout the book, we will be creating and calling a lot of functions.

Libraries

Python libraries are sets of prewritten code that offer practical tools and functions, saving developers the trouble of creating everything from scratch. These libraries make the development process easier by providing premade solutions for a variety of tasks, such as data manipulation and visualization. You can incorporate premade modules and functions from Python libraries into your programs. Errors are decreased, and time is saved. Libraries are frequently made with specific goals in mind. For example:

- **numpy** is used for numerical computations and array processing.
- **pandas** is used for data analysis and data frame manipulation.
- **matplotlib** is used for creating visualizations.

Many Python libraries are open source, meaning they are free to use, modify, and distribute. This encourages community collaboration and the continuous improvement of libraries. Using a library entails installing it and then importing it. Installing a library is equivalent to downloading it using the **pip** command from the Anaconda prompt (not the code editor):

```
pip install -library_name
```

Importing the library is equivalent to telling the editor to be ready to use it (from the code editor):

```
import library_name
# you can also use import library_name as shorter_name for ease of access
```

Using the command **as** gives you the right to nickname the library. For example:

```
import matplotlib.pyplot as plt
```

This will allow you to refer to the library's name as **plt** every time you want to use it.

```
plt.plot(my_data_frame)
# as opposed to matplotlib.pyplot.plot(my_data_frame)
```

Python offers a rich ecosystem of libraries that simplify and enhance data analysis, visualization, and algorithm development. To use libraries, you have to install them and then import them.

Basic Time Series Plotting

The concept of a time series refers to a sequence of data points collected and recorded at regular time intervals. When your parents recorded your height every few months growing up, that formed a hopefully ascending time series. Time series can basically be decomposed into the following:

- The general direction in which the data is moving over a long period. This is also referred to as the trend (or market regime). It can be bullish (rising), bearish (falling), or sideways.
- Regular patterns or cycles in the data that repeat over a specific period (e.g., daily, weekly, yearly). This is also referred to as seasonality.
- Data patterns that occur at irregular intervals, often influenced by economic cycles and technical anomalies.
- Random noise that is not explained by any of the above. Due to the sheer number of participants and exogenous variables, market moves cannot be predicted all the time.

As you have previously seen, OHLC data refers to data that contains open, high, low, and close prices. Let's create a function that allows us to generate 500 hypothetical OHLC data.

```python
def generate_ohlc_data(length_data=1000):
 # create zero-value ohlc arrays
 data = {
  'open': np.zeros(length_data),
  'high': np.zeros(length_data),
  'low': np.zeros(length_data),
  'close': np.zeros(length_data)}
 # initialize the first prices
 data['open'][0] = np.random.uniform(100, 200)
 data['close'][0] = data['open'][0] + np.random. uniform(-5, 5)
 data['high'][0] = max(data['open'][0], data['close'][0]) + np.random.uniform(0, 5)
 data['low'][0] = min(data['open'][0],
data['close'][0]) - np.random.uniform(0, 5)
 # simulate the path of the hypothetical time series
 for i in range(1, length_data):
  data['open'][i] = data['close'][i-1] + np.
  random.uniform(-3, 3)
  data['close'][i] = data['open'][i] + np.random. uniform(-5, 5)
  data['high'][i] = max(data['open'][i], data['close'][i]) + np.random.uniform(0, 5)
  data['low'][i] = min(data['open'][i], data['close'][i]) - np.random.uniform(0, 5)
 # convert to pandas dataframe
 my_time_series = pd.DataFrame(data)
 return my_time_series
```

The concept of using a function is referred to as calling it. If you want to create a new data frame with what the function returns, you can call it as follows.

my_time_series = generate_ohlc_data(length_data=1000)

Now, let's create a function that allows us to chart it through three different means:

- Thin bars chart, which is just a black bars chart to facilitate the visual interpretation
- Candlestick chart, which you have already seen in Chapter 1
- Line chart, which uses the close price only in an effort to simplify the plot

```python
def ohlc_plot(my_time_series, window=250, plot_type='bars', chart_type='ohlc'):
    # choose a sampling window
    sample = my_time_series.iloc[-window:, ]
    # create a plot
    fig, ax = plt.subplots(figsize = (10, 5))
    # thin black bars for better long-term visualization
    if plot_type == 'bars':
        for i in sample.index:
            plt.vlines(x=i, ymin=sample.at[i, 'low'], ymax=sample.at[i, 'high'], color='black', linewidth=1)
            if sample.at[i, 'close'] > sample.at[i, 'open']:
                plt.vlines(x=i, ymin=sample.at[i, 'open'], ymax=sample.at[i, 'close'], color='black',
linewidth=1)
            if sample.at[i, 'close'] < sample.at[i, 'open']:
                plt.vlines(x=i, ymin = sample.at[i, 'close'], ymax=sample.at[i, 'open'], color='black',
linewidth=1)
            if sample.at[i, 'close'] == sample.at[i, 'open']:
                plt.vlines(x=i, ymin = sample.at[i, 'close'], ymax=sample.at[i, 'open']+1, color='black', linewidth=1)
    # regular candlesticks for better interpretation
    elif plot_type == 'candlesticks':
        for i in sample.index:
            plt.vlines(x=i, ymin=sample.at[i, 'low'], ymax=sample.at[i, 'high'], color='black', linewidth=1)
            if sample.at[i, 'close'] > sample.at[i, 'open']:
                plt.vlines(x=i, ymin=sample.at[i, 'open'], ymax=sample.at[i, 'close'], color='green', linewidth=3)
            if sample.at[i, 'close'] < sample.at[i, 'open']:
                plt.vlines(x=i, ymin=sample.at[i, 'close'], ymax=sample.at[i, 'open'], color='red', linewidth=3)
            if sample.at[i, 'close'] == sample.at[i, 'open']:
                plt.vlines(x=i, ymin=sample.at[i, 'close'], ymax=sample.at[i, 'open']+0.5, color='black', linewidth=3)
    # simple line chart using the open prices (to choose close, switch the below argument)
    elif plot_type == 'line':
```

```
 if chart_type == 'ohlc':
   plt.plot(sample['open'], color='black')
 elif chart_type == 'simple_economic_indicator':
   plt.plot(sample['value'], color='black')
 elif chart_type == 'simple_financial':
   plt.plot(sample['close'], color='black')
else:
  print('Choose between bars or candlesticks')
plt.grid()
plt.show()
plt.tight_layout()
```

Visual interpretation helps detect the trend and the nature of the time series. Classic technical analysis relies heavily on the trader's observation and interpretation of the trend and patterns. Use the following code to plot the three different charts (line, bars, and candlesticks).

```
# generate ohlc data
my_time_series = generate_ohlc_data(length_data=250)
# plot bars
ohlc_plot(my_time_series, window=250, plot_type='bars')
# plot candlesticks
ohlc_plot(my_time_series, window=250, plot_type='candlesticks')
# plot line
ohlc_plot(my_time_series, window=250, plot_type='line')
```

Figure 2.3 shows the result of plotting using plot_type='bars'.

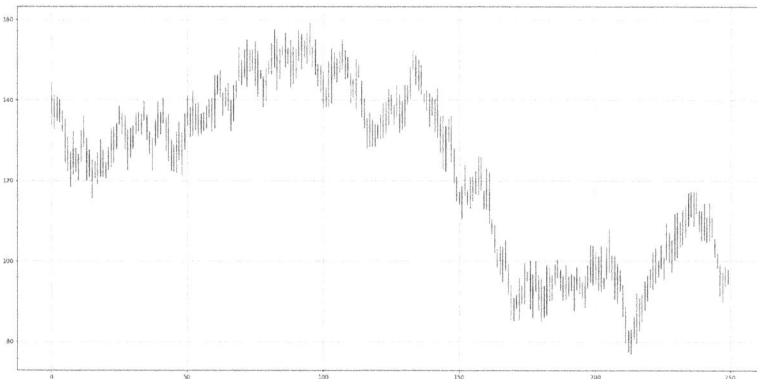

Figure 2.3 A chart showing simple bars

Historical Data Import Methods

This is one of the most important sections, as you will see how to download and import free historical OHLC data. Data is this era's gold, and having instant access to it is paramount to succeed in the world of trading and investing. To maximize your chances of fetching quality data, you will see the following methods, which will all be included in one master function called **import_data()**:

- The Yahoo Finance method (the most used one)
- The MetaTrader method
- The FRED Saint-Louis method
- The manual method

Free OHLC data is crucial, and properly fetching it is extremely helpful to avoid paying for data providers. The first source is Yahoo Finance, with its Python module **yfinance.** The **yfinance** library provides access to financial data. It pulls data from Yahoo Finance, making it easier to gather and analyze market data for financial analysis, algorithmic trading, back-testing, and research. The second importing method requires installing a trading and charting software called MetaTrader 5 and creating a free demo account. You will also have to use the **MT5** module in Python to download data (mostly used for currencies historical data). The next source comes from the Federal Reserve of Saint-Louis' website, which is a great source for economic data. It lacks competitiveness with financial data because it only contains the close price as opposed to the full OHLC offer. Finally, the last source is a simple manual import using an Excel file that you have downloaded or created on your own. The manual method can be used if the previous methods are unavailable. The requirement is to have previously downloaded OHLC data from a third party in a spreadsheet saved on your computer. You can find a selection of predownloaded historical data in the GitHub repository. It is important to **pip install** the required libraries as follows.

```
pip install yfinance
pip install MT5
pip install pandas_datareader
```

Now, import the required functions.

```
import yfinance as yf
import MetaTrader5 as mt5
import datetime
import pytz
import pandas_datareader as pdr
```

The master function **import_data** is a global function that includes a number of third-party data sources. You can find the function in the GitHub repository, as it's too lengthy to be written in the book. The following code block shows a few examples of how to import data from various sources.

```
from master_library import import_data
# import apple daily stock data from yahoo finance
my_time_series_yf = import_data(name='AAPL', start_date='2017-01-01', end_date='2025-06-01',
                    data_provider='yahoo_finance', time_frame='daily')
# import eurusd hourly stock data from metatrader5
my_time_series_mt = import_data(name='EURUSD', start_date='2017-01-01', end_date='2025-06-01',
                    data_provider='metatrader', time_frame='hourly')
# import consumer price index monthly data from fred
my_time_series_fr = import_data(name='CPIAUCSL', start_date='2017-01-01', end_date='2025-06-01',
                    data_provider='fred')
# import tnote-10 etf data manually (xlsx)
my_time_series_xlsx = import_data(name='tnote_10_etf.xlsx', data_provider='manual_import_xlsx')
# import louis vuitton historical data manually (csv)
my_time_series_csv = import_data(name='louis_vuitton.csv', data_provider='manual_import_csv')
```

When importing manually, do not forget to add the **.xlsx** extension to Excel files and the **.csv** extension to CSV files. With functions, when an argument is already set to a default value in the definition, such as **start_date** and **end_date**, there is no need to write it again when calling the function unless you want to change the argument. This explains why it was omitted when importing Apple's stock price and EURUSD values in the previous code block. Notice how **data_provider** was not omitted when importing EURUSD because MetaTrader was used as the data provider instead of the default Yahoo Finance choice.

Miscellaneous Improvements and Common Errors

This section will cover miscellaneous topics to help optimize your code and better understand the reasoning behind errors. Additionally, you will learn to manage imports from local folders.

Handling Exceptions

Python uses exceptions to handle errors during program execution. If your program hits a problem it can't handle, it throws an exception—halting execution unless you deal with it. Understanding how to raise, catch, and manage exceptions is crucial for writing robust, crash-resistant code. An exception is a Python object that signals an error or unusual condition. Common exceptions include ZeroDivisionError, TypeError, ValueError, and IndexError. For example, if you run the following code.

```
print(1 / 0)
```

You will get a ZeroDivisionError. This is because mathematically, division by zero is impossible. However, you can use try and except to catch and respond to exceptions.

```
try:
  print('One divided by one = ', 1/1)
  print('One divided by zero = ', 1/0)
except ZeroDivisionError:
  pass
```

The previous code will print the first statement but not the second one because it didn't satisfy the ZeroDivisionError condition, therefore it was passed. In time series workflows, you often loop through many time points, files, or records. If one item fails (e.g., corrupted data, missing value, or division by zero), you may want to skip it and continue. Additionally, time series data often contains gaps, malformed timestamps, or invalid values. You can avoid crashes by catching and skipping these issues. Also, when quickly testing functions across a large dataset, try-except-pass helps avoid stopping the whole script due to one bad entry. It's worth noting that in risky operations, you may use the following instead of pass, which will point out the error but still continue.

```
try:
  # risky operation
except Exception as e:
  print(f"Error at index {i}: {e}")
  continue
```

Therefore, you can understand and fix the root cause of errors.

Remove Warnings

For aesthetic reasons and only when you are certain of the quality of your code, you may sometimes want to remove the warnings that occur due to deprecation or other nonfatal issues. In that case, you may run this code before you start.

```
import warnings
warnings.filterwarnings("ignore")
```

This will clean the output and show more visually appealing results in the console.

Library Updates

Sometimes your code needs a specific version of a library—either newer or older—to run correctly or avoid compatibility issues. That's where upgrading and downgrading libraries come in. From the Anaconda prompt, if you need to upgrade your library, run the following command.

```
pip install --upgrade library_name
```

If you want to specify the exact version you want (therefore, downgrading or upgrading), use the following command.

```
pip install library_name == 1.3.5
```

To see what version you currently have, use the following command.

```
pip show library_name
```

Avoiding Errors in Library Importing

Importing libraries in Python should be simple, but in practice, it's one of the most common sources of frustration—especially when juggling different environments, versions, or installations. Here's a list of the most common errors when importing libraries:

- **ModuleNotFoundError** occurs when the library isn't installed in your current Python environment. Use **where python** to make sure you're using the same Python/pip environment.
- **ImportError** occurs when you're trying to import something that doesn't exist in that version, or the syntax is wrong. Double-check your spelling and case and make sure you're using the correct version. Additionally, you can check the online documentation for what you're importing.
- You accidentally named your own file the same as a standard or external module. Python imports your file instead of the real module. In this case, you must rename your file (e.g., you should not name it **pandas.py**).
- Some libraries only work in certain Python versions. In this case, you must check your version through this prompt command: **python –version**.

The most important part is to fully understand the data importing part. First, the **import_data()** function allows you to have a few external data sources from which to download historical data. Second, in case you prefer to use your own data, you can use the manual import method as explained previously. Additionally, in the GitHub repository, you can find ready-to-import files containing different historical data for you to use and apply the concepts seen in the book. All you need to do is to download the files, set the Python directory path accordingly, and choose the manual import by setting the argument **data_provider** to **'manual_import'**.

Importing Functions from master_library

Many of the functions you will encounter throughout the chapters are found in **master_library.py**, a custom Python library that we frequently make use of in this book. We import only the necessary functions into each program and group related functions into a single file to keep the code neat and orderly. If you only require specific functions (e.g., **generate _ohlc_data** and **moving_average**), you can import them in this way:

```
from master_library import moving_average, generate_ohlc_data
```

This makes it obvious what dependencies your code has because only the designated functions are added to your current program. As an alternative, if you wish to access everything in the library, you can import it all:

```
import master_library
```

In this case, you would call functions using the master_library. prefix:

```
master_library.generate_ohlc_data (my_time_series)
```

For these imports to work, the master_library.py file needs to be in the same directory as the Python script you're running. For example:

```
project_folder/
|
├──── master_library.py
└──── your_program.py
```

If your files are organized this way, Python will be able to locate **master_library.py** automatically. If you prefer, you can run the **master_library. py** file once in your Python environment. This will define all functions in the current namespace, so you can use them without any import statements. However, using **import** is usually a better practice, as it keeps your code modular and easier to maintain.

CHAPTER 3

Modern Technical Analysis Techniques and Indicators

This chapter serves as a preamble to more advanced topics. The primary goal is to present a number of alternative technical indicators and methods that are not always under the spotlight, despite being useful. First, we'll go over a number of exotic moving averages that should be at the forefront of your market analysis. After that, we'll cover some fresh techniques for using time-tested indicators like the RSI and Bollinger bands. Subsequently, the rainbow collection, consisting of seven personal technical indicators that use different techniques and indicators to predict market reactions, will be discussed.

Exotic Moving Averages

By now, you are familiar with the simple moving average (SMA) after seeing it in Chapter 1, but there are other types of moving averages to discover and use. They are more complex than a simple division of the sum by the quantity. In this section, you will see the following:

- The weighted moving average
- The inverse weighted moving average
- The Hull moving average
- The adaptive moving average
- The Arnaud Legoux moving average
- The ordinary least squares moving average
- Honorable mentions

The Weighted Moving Average

The weighted moving average (WMA) places more importance on re-cent data points compared to older ones. This makes the WMA more responsive to changes in data trends compared to the SMA, which treats all data points equally. In a WMA, different weights are assigned to each data point. The most recent data points have the highest weights, and these weights decrease as you go back in time. The WMA is calculated by multiplying each data point by its assigned weight and then summing up the weighted values. This sum is then divided by the sum of the weights to get the final WMA value. Let's see how to calculate the WMA:

1. Assign weights to each data point. Typically, more recent data points get higher weights. For example, if you have three data points, you might assign their weights as $w_1 = 1$, $w_2 = 2$, and $w_3 = 3$. The sum of the different weights would therefore be 6.
4. Multiply each data point by its respective weight, then add up the weighted values.
5. Divide the sum of the weighted values by the sum of the weights to get the WMA.

Consider the following chronologically ordered time series {10, 20, 30} with weights {1, 2, 3}. Suppose you want to calculate the WMA. The steps you must follow are as follows:

1. Calculate the weighted values:

$$10 \times 1 = 10$$
$$20 \times 2 = 40$$
$$30 \times 3 = 90$$

2. Sum the weighted values:

$$10 + 40 + 90 = 140$$

3. Sum the weight

$$1 + 2 + 3 = 6$$

4. Calculate the WMA as the sum of the weighted values divided by the sum of the weighted values:

$$WMA = \frac{140}{6} \approx 23.33$$

By contrast, the SMA would be 20, which would reflect less the recent reality. For illustration, the following is the SMA's formula given the same example:

$$SMA = \frac{10 + 20 + 30}{3} = 20$$

The WMA reflects recent changes in the trend better than the SMA does due to its calculation method. Calculating the WMA is a bit more complex, but that shouldn't be a problem nowadays with the availability of indicators and code. It is also important to note that because recent data points have more weight, outliers can have a more significant impact on the WMA than on the SMA. The following function defines the WMA for a given data frame.

```python
def wma(my_time_series, source='close', ma_lookback=50):
    # generate weights based on the lookback period
    weights = np.arange(1, ma_lookback + 1)
    # create an empty series to store WMA values
    my_time_series['WMA'] = 0
    # compute WMA for each rolling window
    for i in range(ma_lookback - 1, len(my_time_series)):
        window = my_time_series[source].iloc[i - ma_lookback + 1:i + 1]
        weighted_sum = np.dot(window, weights)
        sum_of_weights = weights.sum()
        my_time_series['WMA'].iloc[i] = weighted_sum / sum_of_weights
    return my_time_series['WMA'].dropna()
```

Figure 3.1 shows an application of the WMA compared to a benchmark SMA for the same lookback period (window) set by **ma_lookback** as 50.

Figure 3.1 **WMA** *versus* **SMA** (dashed)

The Inverse Weighted Moving Average

The inverse weighted moving average (IWMA) is a variation of the WMA where the most recent data points are given less weight, and the older data points are given more weight. This approach is less common than the standard WMA, but can be useful in specific scenarios where historical data is considered more relevant than recent data. In an IWMA, the weights are assigned in reverse order compared to a standard WMA. The oldest data point receives the highest weight, and the most recent data point receives the lowest weight. The IWMA is useful when you want to focus on long-term trends and give less importance to short-term fluctuations. It can provide a smoother average in scenarios where recent data is volatile or considered less reliable. In some cases, you might want to compare recent data to long-term trends, and IWMA helps in such analyses by highlighting deviations from established patterns. It is important to note, however, that IWMA is slower to react to recent changes, which might be a disadvantage in situations where recent data is more relevant, such as a trend shift. The following function defines the IWMA for a given data frame.

```
def iwma(my_time_series, source='close', ma_lookback=50):
    # generate weights based on the lookback period
    weights = np.arange(1, ma_lookback + 1)[::-1]
    # create an empty series to store IWMA values
    my_time_series['IWMA'] = 0
    # compute IWMA for each rolling window
    for i in range(ma_lookback - 1, len(my_time_series)):
        window = my_time_series[source].iloc[i - ma_lookback + 1:i + 1]
        weighted_sum = np.dot(window, weights)
        sum_of_weights = weights.sum()
        my_time_series['IWMA'].iloc[i] = weighted_sum / sum_of_weights
    return my_time_series['IWMA'].dropna()
```

Figure 3.2 shows an application of the IWMA compared to an SMA for the same lookback.

It is also interesting to know that you can use a moving average cross strategy using the WMA and the IWMA with the same lookback period, thus removing one parameter from the strategy (the first parameter

Figure 3.2 IWMA *versus* SMA (dashed)

being the short moving average and the second parameter being the long moving average). The default moving average cross strategy has the following rules:

- A bullish signal is generated whenever the short-term moving average crosses over the long-term moving average.
- A bearish signal is generated whenever the short-term moving average crosses under the long-term moving average.

The strategy generally implies that we need to have two lookback periods (windows). The first lookback is the short-term moving average, and the second lookback is the long-term moving average. However, with the WMA and IWMA, we can circumvent this by considering one lookback period for both, and considering the WMA as the short-term moving average and the IWMA as the long-term moving average. Figure 3.3 shows the WMA and the IWMA applied to the Russell 2000 index. Notice how a bullish signal can be generated whenever the WMA crosses over the IWMA, while a bearish signal can be generated whenever the WMA crosses under the IWMA.

As the WMA rises above the IWMA, a bullish signal is generated in anticipation of a strengthening bullish trend. In contrast, as the WMA dips below the IWMA, a bearish signal is generated in anticipation of a bearish trend.

Figure 3.3 WMA (dashed) *versus* IWMA

The Hull Moving Average

Let's hover over the next moving average. The Hull moving average (HMA) is a type of moving average designed to reduce the lag associated with traditional moving averages (e.g., SMA) while enhancing the smoothing of the data. It achieves this by combining WMAs in a specific way. The HMA was developed by Alan Hull, and it is particularly popular for its ability to provide a smooth and responsive average that is less affected by short-term fluctuations. The HMA reduces the lag by using a weighted average of two WMAs—one calculated over a shorter period and one over a longer period. The HMA is much smoother than a traditional moving average, and it reacts more rapidly to changes in the data trend. This makes it particularly useful in situations where you want to minimize lag but still need to filter out noise. Despite being responsive, the HMA provides a smooth line, avoiding the choppiness that can come with more reactive moving averages. The final step of the HMA involves applying another WMA to smooth the result further. Follow these steps:

1. Calculate a WMA using half the chosen lookback period.
2. Calculate a WMA using the full lookback period.
3. Combine both WMAs in the following way:

$$\text{Combined WMA} = \text{WMA}\left(\frac{n}{2}\right) \times 2 - \text{WMA}(n)$$

4. Calculate the WMA of the result over the square root of the period.

$$HMA = WMA(\text{Combined } WMA, \sqrt{n})$$

The following code shows how to create a function that outputs the HMA for a given data frame.

```
def hma(my_time_series, ma_lookback=50):
  # half period WMA as integer
  half_lookback = ma_lookback // 2
  # calculate WMA for half period
  my_time_series['WMA_half'] = wma(my_time_series,
ma_lookback=half_lookback)
  # calculate WMA for full period
  my_time_series['WMA_full'] = wma(my_time_series,
ma_lookback=ma_lookback)
  # HMA calculation
  my_time_series['HMA_numerator'] = 2 * my_time_series['WMA_half']
- my_time_series['WMA_full']
  hma_lookback = int(np.sqrt(ma_lookback))
  my_time_series['HMA'] = wma(my_time_series, source='HMA_numera-
tor', ma_lookback=hma_lookback)
  # drop the initial columns as they are not needed anymore
  my_time_series.drop(['WMA_half', 'WMA_full', 'HMA_numerator'], axis=1,
inplace=True)
  return my_time_series.dropna()
```

Figure 3.4 shows the HMA with the SMA of the same lookback period as a comparison.

Figure 3.4 HMA versus SMA (dashed)

The performance of HMA can vary significantly based on the choice of the lookback period (window), and finding the optimal value may require some trial and error. The HMA offers a balance between responsiveness and smoothness, making it a valuable tool in scenarios where both qualities are important. From Figure 3.4, it is clear that the HMA outperforms the SMA in terms of responsiveness. It may also be interesting to know that by default, when you import a function from a file that requires a library and that library is imported in the **master_library.py** file, it will get imported, so there is no need to redefine it in the current script. For example, the **hma()** function requires the use of the **wma()** function. However, in your script, you only need to import **hma** from **master_library.py**.

The Adaptive Moving Average

Also known as the Kaufman adaptive moving average (KAMA), this overlay indicator adapts to market conditions by adjusting its smoothing factor based on the volatility of the price or data series. Developed by Perry Kaufman, KAMA is particularly useful in financial markets as it can adapt to different market conditions, becoming more responsive in trending markets and less responsive in choppy, sideways markets. KAMA adjusts its smoothing factor based on the level of noise (volatility) in the data. When the data series is trending, KAMA will respond more quickly; when the data is noisy, it will smooth out the fluctuations more. KAMA uses an efficiency ratio (ER) to determine the degree of trendiness in the data. ER measures the ratio of the total price movement to the sum of the absolute price changes over a certain period. The smoothing factor in KAMA changes based on ER. This is what allows KAMA to adapt to different market conditions. Let's discuss the calculation steps:

1. Calculate ER using this formula:

$$ER = \frac{|\operatorname{Price}_i - \operatorname{price}_{i-n}|}{\sum_{i=0}^{n-1} |\operatorname{Price}_i - \operatorname{price}_{i-1}|}$$

2. Calculate smoothing constant (SC) using this formula:

$$SC = [ER \times (fastest\ SC - slowest\ SC) + slowest\ SC]^2$$

3. In the previous step, the fastest SC typically uses a period of 2 (corresponding to a smoothing factor for a 2-period exponential moving average [EMA]), and the slowest SC uses a period of 30 (corresponding to a smoothing factor for a 30-period EMA). Next, calculate KAMA using the following formula:

$$KAMA_i = KAMA_{i-1} + SC \times (price_i - KAMA_{i-1})$$

KAMA automatically adjusts its sensitivity based on the level of noise or volatility in the data, making it suitable for various market conditions.

- In trending markets, KAMA is more responsive, reducing the lag that is common with traditional moving averages.
- In sideways or choppy markets, KAMA smooths out the noise, providing a more reliable signal.

KAMA's ability to adapt dynamically makes it a powerful tool in situations where market conditions or data patterns are expected to change frequently. It is especially useful in financial markets for trading strategies that need to respond to varying levels of volatility. The following code block shows how to develop a KAMA function.

```
def kama(my_time_series, source='close', ma_lookback=50, fastest=2,
slowest=30):
  def kaufman_er(my_time_series, source='close', er_lookback=20):
    change = abs(my_time_series[source].diff(er_lookback))
    volatility = my_time_series[source].diff().abs().rolling(window=er_look-
back).sum()
    er = change / volatility
    return er
  # calculate the ER using the previous function
  er = kaufman_er(my_time_series, source='close', er_lookback=20)
  # calculate the SC
  fastest_sc = 2 / (fastest + 1)
```

```
slowest_sc = 2 / (slowest + 1)
sc = (er * (fastest_sc - slowest_sc) + slowest_sc) ** 2
# initialize KAMA series with NaN
my_time_series['KAMA'] = pd.Series(np.nan, index=my_time_series.
index)
# start KAMA calculation from the first available data point
my_time_series['KAMA'].iloc[ma_lookback] = my_time_series[source].
iloc[ma_lookback]
# calculate KAMA iteratively
for i in range(ma_lookback + 1, len(my_time_series[source])):
    my_time_series['KAMA'].iloc[i] = my_time_series['KAMA'].iloc[i-1] + \
            sc.iloc[i] * (my_time_series[source].iloc[i] - \
            my_time_series['KAMA'].iloc[i-1])
return my_time_series.dropna()
```

ER indicates the market's trending strength, with values closer to 1 indicating a strong trend and values closer to 0 indicating more noise. Using ER, the function calculates the SC, which is used to adapt the moving average. The SC is derived from the fastest and slowest periods provided, allowing KAMA to adjust its sensitivity based on market conditions. Figure 3.5 shows KAMA with the SMA of the same lookback period as a comparison.

Figure 3.5 KAMA *versus* SMA (dashed)

The Arnaud Legoux Moving Average

Arnaud Legoux moving average (ALMA) is a type of moving average that aims to minimize lag while enhancing smoothness. It does so by applying a Gaussian (bell-shaped) weighting function to the data series, which results in a smoother and more responsive moving average. ALMA was developed by Arnaud Legoux and Dimitrios Kouzis-Loukas. The ALMA applies a Gaussian weighting function to the data, giving more importance to data points near the center of the window and less to those at the edges. This weighting reduces the influence of outliers and provides a smoother average. It includes an offset parameter that shifts the center of the Gaussian curve, allowing the user to control the balance between lag and responsiveness. Like other moving averages, the window size determines the number of periods over which the average is calculated. However, in ALMA, the Gaussian weights are distributed within this window. Let's walk through the process of calculating the ALMA:

1. Compute the weights for the moving average using a Gaussian distribution:

$$\text{Weight}_i = e^{\left(-\frac{(i-\mu)^2}{2\sigma^2} \right)}$$

2. Normalize the weights so that their sum equals 1:

$$\text{Weights} = \frac{\text{Weights}}{\text{Sum of weights}}$$

3. Multiply each price in the window by its corresponding weight and sum the results:

$$\text{ALMA}_t = \sum_{i=0}^{N-1} \text{Weight}(i) \times \text{price}(t - N + i)$$

The Gaussian weighting function smooths the data more effectively, reducing the impact of outliers. The following code block shows how to create the ALMA in Python:

```
def alma(my_time_series, source='close', ma_lookback=50, offset=0.85, sigma=3):
    # initialize the weights array
    m = offset * (ma_lookback - 1)
    s = ma_lookback / sigma
    weights = np.exp(-((np.arange(ma_lookback) - m) ** 2) / (2 * s ** 2))
    weights /= np.sum(weights)
    # calculate ALMA
    my_time_series['ALMA'] = ''
    my_time_series['ALMA'] = my_time_series[source].rolling(ma_lookback).apply(lambda x: np.dot(x, weights), raw=True)
    return my_time_series.dropna()
```

Figure 3.6 shows the ALMA in action compared to a similar SMA.

Figure 3.6 ALMA *versus* SMA (dashed)

The Least Squares Moving Average

The least squares moving average (LSMA) fits a straight line over a fixed window of past data using least squares, then takes the last point (rightmost on a chart) on that fitted line as the indicator value. Suppose you have a time series y and a window size N to calculate LSMA follow these two steps:

1. Fit a line $y_i = \beta_0 + \beta_1 x_i$ where:

$$x_i = 1, 2, ..., N$$
$$y_i = y[t - N + i]$$

2. Use the fitted model to compute the value at $x = N$ (the last point in the window). This will give you LSMA at time t.

Use the following code to implement the LSMA in Python.

```
def lsma(my_time_series, ma_lookback=50):
    my_time_series_copy = np.asarray(my_time_series)
    n = len(my_time_series_copy)
    lsma = np.full(n, np.nan)
    x = np.arange(1, ma_lookback+1)
    X = np.vstack([np.ones(ma_lookback), x]).T
    for t in range(ma_lookback - 1, n):
```

```
   y_window = my_time_series_copy[t-ma_lookback + 1 : t+1, 3]
   beta, *_ = np.linalg.lstsq(X, y_window, rcond=None)
   lsma_value = beta[0] + beta[1] * ma_lookback
   lsma[t] = lsma_value
 lsma = pd.DataFrame(lsma)
 my_time_series['LSMA'] = lsma.values
 return my_time_series.dropna()
```

Figure 3.7 shows the LSMA in action compared to an SMA.

Figure 3.7 LSMA *versus* SMA (dashed)

The LSMA can capture local trends instead of assuming the mean is flat, such as in an SMA. The result is often smoother and better adapted to the underlying signal than that of SMA.

Honorable Mentions

This section will cover two other types of moving averages that you must be aware of, despite them not being exotic. The first is the EMA. EMA is a type of moving average that places greater weight on the most recent data points, making it more responsive to recent price changes compared to SMA. The core intuition behind EMA is that market participants often care more about what's happening now than what happened weeks ago. By emphasizing recent prices, EMA captures shifts in momentum or trend faster, which can be useful in volatile markets or for short-term trading strategies. Unlike SMA, which averages a fixed set of past values equally, EMA uses a smoothing factor to apply exponentially decreasing weights to older data.

$$EMA_t = \alpha.y_t + (1 - \alpha).EMA_{t-1}$$

The smoothing factor α is a crucial parameter in the EMA calculation, as it controls how quickly the EMA responds to changes in the data. A higher α makes EMA more responsive to recent changes, while a lower α makes it more stable and smoother. It is worth noting that α can be calculated based on the chosen lookback period n for EMA:

$$\alpha = \frac{2}{n+1}$$

The other type of moving average is the smoothed moving average (SMMA[5]), also known as the moving average used in the RSI. It is similar to EMA, but it updates more slowly and uses a different smoothing approach. SMMA is simply an EMA with a higher lookback period. The following shows the transformation process:

$$Lookback_{SMMA} = (Lookback_{EMA} \times 2) - 1$$

Therefore, a 5-period SMMA is equivalent to a 9-period EMA. The following code is a generalized moving average code that allows you to choose the type of moving average you want to output between {SMA, EMA, SMMA}.

```
def moving_average(my_time_series, source='close', ma_lookback=200, output_name='moving_average', ma_type='SMA'):
    '''
    The moving averages available in this function:
        * Simple moving average (SMA)
        * Exponential moving average (EMA)
        * Smoothed moving average (SMMA)
    '''
    if source not in my_time_series.columns:
        raise ValueError(f"Column '{source}' not found in DataFrame, choose SMA, EMA, or SMMA")
    # calculate the simple moving average
    if ma_type == 'SMA':
        my_time_series[output_name] = my_time_series[source].rolling(window=ma_lookback).mean()
        return my_time_series.dropna()
    # calculate the exponential moving average
```

---

[5] The smoothed moving average is commonly referred to as SMMA instead of SMA to differentiate it from the simple moving average (SMA).

```
elif ma_type == 'EMA':
  my_time_series[output_name] = my_time_series[source].ewm(span=ma_lookback, adjust=False).mean()
  return my_time_series.dropna()
# calculate the smoothed moving average
elif ma_type == 'SMMA':
  my_time_series[output_name] = my_time_series[source].ewm(span=(ma_lookback*2)-1, adjust=False).mean()
  return my_time_series.dropna()
else:
  raise ValueError("ma_type must be either 'SMA', 'EMA', or 'SMMA'")
```

Figure 3.8 shows the three moving averages (SMA, EMA, and SMMA) with the same lookback period. You can see that EMA is the most reactive one and the most suited to follow the trend.

Figure 3.8 EMA versus SMA (dashed) versus SMMA (dotted)

In contrast, SMA and SMMA are more suited to find dynamic support and resistance levels due to their stability.

New Techniques on Bollinger Bands

The main function of Bollinger bands is to envelop the market in order to provide dynamic support and resistance levels, but what are they? Bollinger bands are a technical analysis tool developed by John Bollinger to measure market volatility and identify overbought and oversold conditions. They consist of three lines:

- Middle band: This is a 20-period SMA applied to the close price.
- Upper band: This represents the dynamic resistance and is calculated as the result of the moving average plus the product of a

multiplier and the rolling standard deviation of the price. Mathematically, it can be represented as follows:

$$\text{Upper band} = SMA + (k.STD)$$

- Lower band: This represents the dynamic support and is calculated as the result of the moving average minus the product of a multiplier and the rolling standard deviation of the price. Mathematically, it can be represented as follows:

$$\text{Lower band} = SMA - (k.STD)$$

You will learn about the concept of standard deviation in detail in Chapter 6. Use the following function to create Bollinger bands given a time series.

```
def bollinger_bands(my_time_series, source='close', bb_lookback=20, num_std_dev=2):
    # calculate the moving average
    my_time_series['middle_band'] = my_time_series[source].rolling(window=bb_lookback).mean()
    # calculate the rolling standard deviation
    my_time_series['volatility'] = my_time_series[source].rolling(window=bb_lookback).std()
    # calculate the upper bollinger band
    my_time_series['upper_band'] = my_time_series['middle_band'] + (my_time_series['volatility'] * num_std_dev)
    # calculate the lower bollinger band
    my_time_series['lower_band'] = my_time_series['middle_band'] - (my_time_series['volatility'] * num_std_dev)
    # drop the rolling standard deviation column as it's not typically needed
    my_time_series.drop(['volatility'], axis=1, inplace=True)
    return my_time_series.dropna()
```

Figure 3.9 shows the bands applied to a time series.

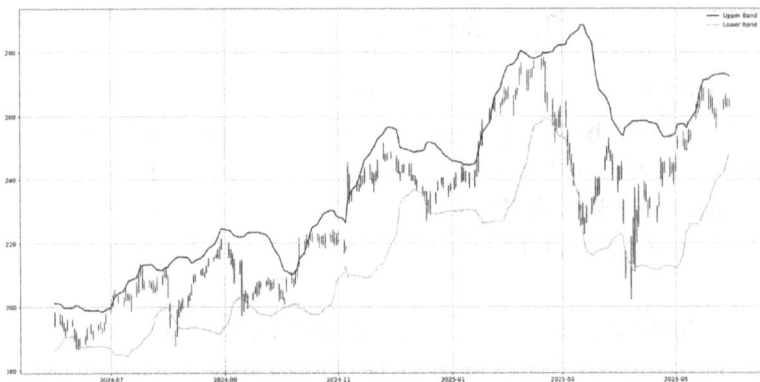

Figure 3.9 Bollinger bands

By default, the go-to technique to use with the Bollinger bands is the aggressive technique. It has the following rules:

- A bullish signal is generated whenever the market crosses below the lower band.
- A bearish signal is generated whenever the market crosses above the upper band.

The following code block shows how to create the aggressive technique in Python:

```python
def bb_aggressive_technique(my_time_series, bb_lookback=20, num_std_dev=2):
  my_time_series = bollinger_bands(my_time_series, source='close', bb_lookback=bb_lookback,
num_std_dev=num_std_dev)
  my_time_series['bullish_signal'] = 0
  my_time_series['bearish_signal'] = 0
  for i in range(0, len(my_time_series)):
    # bullish signal
    if my_time_series['close'].iloc[i] < my_time_series['lower_band'].iloc[i] and \
    my_time_series['close'].iloc[i-1] > my_time_series['lower_band'].iloc[i-1]:
      my_time_series.at[my_time_series.index[i+1], 'bullish_signal'] = 1
    # bearish signal
    elif my_time_series['close'].iloc[i] > my_time_series['upper_band'].iloc[i] and \
    my_time_series['close'].iloc[i-1] < my_time_series['upper_band'].iloc[i-1]:
      my_time_series.at[my_time_series.index[i+1], 'bearish_signal'] = 1
  return my_time_series
```

Figure 3.10 marks the beginning of what we will refer to throughout this book as signal charts.

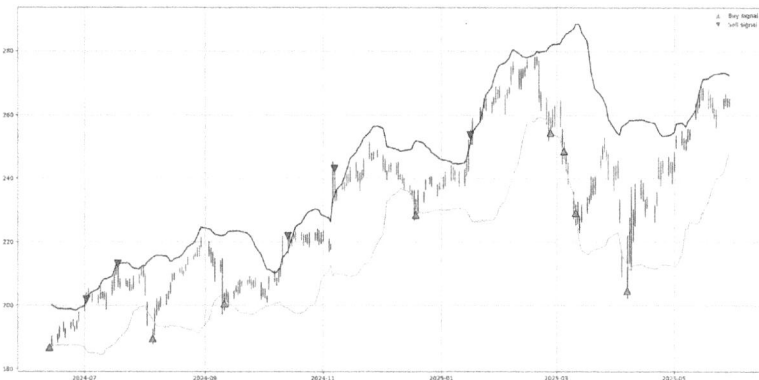

Figure 3.10 Aggressive technique using Bollinger bands

These are standard candlestick or bar charts, augmented with bullish signals (represented by upwards pointing arrows) and bearish signals (represented by downwards pointing arrows). Each signal is plotted on the next open price following the condition's confirmation. For example, if a bullish condition is met at the close of a candle, the green arrow will appear on the following bar's open price—ensuring that the signal is both realistic and replicable in actual trading conditions. The signal chart is defined as follows:

```
def signal_chart(my_time_series, window, choice='bars', source='open', chart_type='ohlc'):
  # choose a sampling window
  sample = my_time_series.iloc[-window:, ]
  if chart_type == 'ohlc':
    ohlc_plot(sample, window, plot_type=choice)
    for i in my_time_series.index:
      if my_time_series.loc[i, 'bullish_signal'] == 1:
        plt.annotate('', xy=(i, my_time_series.loc[i, source]), xytext=(i, my_time_series.loc[i, source]-1),
            arrowprops=dict(facecolor='green', shrink=0.05))
      elif my_time_series.loc[i, 'bearish_signal'] == 1:
        plt.annotate('', xy=(i, my_time_series.loc[i, source]), xytext=(i, my_time_series.loc[i, source]+1),
            arrowprops=dict(facecolor='red', shrink=0.05))
  elif chart_type == 'simple':
    ohlc_plot(sample, window, plot_type = 'line', chart_type='simple')
    for i in my_time_series.index:
      if my_time_series.loc[i, 'bullish_signal'] == 1:
        plt.annotate('', xy=(i, my_time_series.loc[i, source]), xytext=(i, my_time_series.loc[i, source]-1),
            arrowprops=dict(facecolor='green', shrink=0.05))
      elif my_time_series.loc[i, 'bearish_signal'] == 1:
        plt.annotate('', xy=(i, my_time_series.loc[i, source]), xytext=(i, my_time_series.loc[i, source]+1),
            arrowprops=dict(facecolor='red', shrink=0.05))
  from matplotlib.lines import Line2D
  bullish_signal = Line2D([0], [0], marker='^', color='w', label='Buy signal', markerfacecolor='green', markersize=10)
  bearish_signal = Line2D([0], [0], marker='v', color='w', label='Sell signal', markerfacecolor='red', markersize=10)
  plt.legend(handles=[bullish_signal, bearish_signal])
  plt.tight_layout()
```

As you see, the **signal_chart** function builds on the **ohlc_plot** function. Signal charts make it easy to see where and when buy/sell signals occurred. They help verify the effectiveness of a strategy by overlaying signals directly on price action. They also aid in understanding signal behavior within the context of price structure. Figure 3.10 shows the signal chart of the aggressive technique.

The Conservative Technique

Additionally, another technique known as the conservative technique can be applied. It has the following trading rules:

- A bullish signal is generated whenever the market crosses over the lower band.
- A bearish signal is generated whenever the market crosses under the upper band.

Therefore, it is more prudent than the aggressive technique as it awaits the exit from the extreme levels (above the upper band or below the lower band). The following code shows how to implement the conservative technique.

```
def bb_conservative_technique(my_time_series, bb_lookback=20, num_std_dev=2):
  my_time_series = bollinger_bands(my_time_series, source='close', bb_lookback=bb_lookback,
num_std_dev=num_std_dev)
  my_time_series['bullish_signal'] = 0
  my_time_series['bearish_signal'] = 0
  for i in range(0, len(my_time_series)):
    # bullish signal
    if my_time_series['close'].iloc[i] > my_time_series['lower_band'].iloc[i] and \
      my_time_series['close'].iloc[i] < my_time_series['middle_band'].iloc[i] and \
      my_time_series['close'].iloc[i-1] < my_time_series['lower_band'].iloc[i-1]:
      my_time_series.at[my_time_series.index[i+1], 'bullish_signal'] = 1
    # bearish signal
    elif my_time_series['close'].iloc[i] < my_time_series['upper_band'].iloc[i] and \
      my_time_series['close'].iloc[i] > my_time_series['middle_band'].iloc[i] and \
      my_time_series['close'].iloc[i-1] > my_time_series['upper_band'].iloc[i-1]:
      my_time_series.at[my_time_series.index[i+1], 'bearish_signal'] = 1
  return my_time_series
```

In addition to the different rules, the conservative technique imposes that for a bullish signal to be valid, the crossover of the lower band must not extend to the middle band (which is, by default, the 20-period moving average). This also applies to bearish signals. This conservative approach is less likely to trigger false signals compared to the aggressive technique. It waits for the price to show signs of stabilization after crossing the Bollinger bands before generating a signal, aiming for more reliable entry and exit points. Figure 3.11 shows the signal chart of the conservative technique.

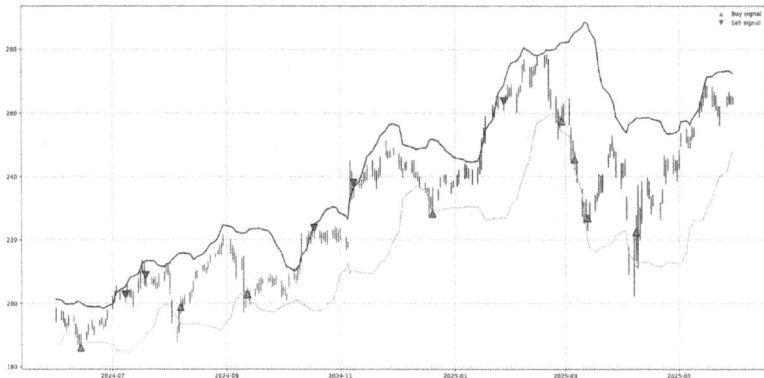

Figure 3.11 Conservative technique using Bollinger bands

The Trend-Friendly Technique

The intuition of this technique is simple; only take bullish conservative signals when the market is trending upward, and only take bearish conservative signals when the market is trending downward. Objectively, you can formulate the algorithm this way:

- A bullish signal is generated whenever the market crosses over the lower band while simultaneously being above the 100-period SMA.
- A bearish signal is generated whenever the market crosses under the upper band while simultaneously being below the 100-period SMA.

The following code shows how to apply the trend-friendly technique in Python:

```
def bb_trend_friendly(my_time_series, bb_lookback=20, ma_lookback=200, num_std_dev=2):
    my_time_series = bollinger_bands(my_time_series, source='close', bb_lookback=bb_lookback,
num_std_dev=num_std_dev)
    my_time_series = moving_average(my_time_series, source='close', ma_lookback=ma_lookback,
output_name='moving_average', ma_type='SMA')
    my_time_series['bullish_signal'] = 0
    my_time_series['bearish_signal'] = 0
```

```
for i in range(0, len(my_time_series)):
  # bullish signal
  if my_time_series['low'].iloc[i] < my_time_series['lower_band'].iloc[i] and \
    my_time_series['low'].iloc[i-1] < my_time_series['lower_band'].iloc[i-1] and \
    my_time_series['low'].iloc[i] > my_time_series['moving_average'].iloc[i-10]:
    my_time_series.at[my_time_series.index[i+1], 'bullish_signal'] = 1
  # bearish signal
  elif my_time_series['high'].iloc[i] > my_time_series['upper_band'].iloc[i] and \
    my_time_series['high'].iloc[i-1] > my_time_series['upper_band'].iloc[i-1] and \
    my_time_series['high'].iloc[i] < my_time_series['moving_average'].iloc[i-10]:
    my_time_series.at[my_time_series.index[i+1], 'bearish_signal'] = 1
return my_time_series
```

Figure 3.12 shows the technique in action.

Figure 3.12 Trend-friendly technique using Bollinger bands

The Bollinger Bands–RSI Overlay Technique

The fourth technique entails the application of Bollinger bands as an overlay on other technical indicators, notably the RSI. By applying Bollinger bands on the RSI, we can get a sense of the statistical extremes over this indicator, which will give reversal signals even when it's not around the oversold and overbought levels. Therefore, this technique increases the frequency of the signals.

```
def bb_rsi_overlay(my_time_series, bb_lookback=20, num_std_dev=2):
  my_time_series = rsi(my_time_series, source='close', output_name='RSI', rsi_lookback=14)
  my_time_series = bollinger_bands(my_time_series, source='RSI', bb_lookback=bb_lookback,
num_std_dev=num_std_dev)
  my_time_series['bullish_signal'] = 0
  my_time_series['bearish_signal'] = 0
  for i in range(0, len(my_time_series)):
    # bullish signal
```

```
if my_time_series['RSI'].iloc[i] > my_time_series['lower_band'].iloc[i] and \
    my_time_series['RSI'].iloc[i-1] < my_time_series['lower_band'].iloc[i-1]:
    my_time_series.at[my_time_series.index[i+1], 'bullish_signal'] = 1
    # bearish signal
elif my_time_series['RSI'].iloc[i] < my_time_series['upper_band'].iloc[i] and \
    my_time_series['RSI'].iloc[i-1] > my_time_series['upper_band'].iloc[i-1]:
    my_time_series.at[my_time_series.index[i+1], 'bearish_signal'] = 1
return my_time_series
```

Figure 3.13 shows the technique in action.

Figure 3.13 RSI overlay technique using Bollinger bands

It is also important to talk about the bands' limitations. For example, Bollinger bands are based on moving averages, which are inherently lagging indicators. This means that they reflect past price data and may not always provide timely signals for future price movements. As a result, we might receive delayed signals that could cause us to miss optimal entry or exit points. In strongly trending markets, prices can stay near the upper or lower band for extended periods without necessarily signaling a reversal. It is up to you to choose how you use Bollinger bands.

New Techniques on the RSI

You have previously seen the RSI in Chapter 1 and understood how it's calculated. The aggressive technique on the RSI has the following rules:

- A bullish signal is generated whenever the RSI crosses under the oversold level.

- A bearish signal is generated whenever the RSI crosses above the overbought level.

The following code block shows how to create the aggressive technique in Python.

```python
def rsi_aggressive_technique(my_time_series, column='close',
output_name='RSI',
                rsi_lookback=14, lower_barrier=30, upper_barrier=70):
  my_time_series = rsi(my_time_series, column, output_name,
rsi_lookback=rsi_lookback)
  my_time_series['bullish_signal'] = 0
  my_time_series['bearish_signal'] = 0
  for i in range(0, len(my_time_series)):
    # bullish signal
    if my_time_series['RSI'].iloc[i] < lower_barrier and \
      my_time_series['RSI'].iloc[i-1] > lower_barrier:
      my_time_series.at[my_time_series.index[i+1], 'bullish_signal'] = 1
    # bearish signal
    elif my_time_series['RSI'].iloc[i] > upper_barrier and \
      my_time_series['RSI'].iloc[i-1] < upper_barrier:
      my_time_series.at[my_time_series.index[i+1], 'bearish_signal'] = 1
  return my_time_series
```

Figure 3.14 shows signals generated from the aggressive RSI technique.

Figure 3.14 Aggressive technique using RSI

For many years of studying the RSI, I have found that there are other techniques you can deploy on the RSI to get a proper market signal. In this section, I will present three techniques that can help you diversify your RSI usage. Meanwhile, try coding the conservative technique on the RSI by yourself. Figure 3.15 shows a signal chart on the RSI using the conservative technique.

Figure 3.15 *Conservative technique using RSI*

The V Technique

The V technique, as the name suggests, refers to instances where the RSI shapes a V or Λ configuration around the oversold and overbought levels, respectively, while keeping in mind certain conditions. The hypothesis of this technique is that the RSI is less likely to stick to the extreme levels, and therefore should coincide with a better market reaction. The trading rules of the V technique are as follows:

- A bullish signal is generated whenever the RSI breaks the oversold level and then surpasses it in the next close, thus shaping a V figure.
- A bearish signal is generated whenever the RSI surpasses the overbought level and then breaks it in the next close, thus shaping a Λ figure.

The following code shows how to implement the V technique.

```
def v_technique(my_time_series, column='close', output_name='RSI', rsi_lookback=5, lower_barrier=15,
upper_barrier=85):
    my_time_series = rsi(my_time_series, column, output_name, rsi_lookback=rsi_lookback)
```

```
my_time_series['bullish_signal'] = 0
my_time_series['bearish_signal'] = 0
for i in range(0, len(my_time_series)):
  # bullish signal
  if my_time_series['RSI'].iloc[i] > lower_barrier and my_time_series['RSI'].iloc[i] < 50 and \
    my_time_series['RSI'].iloc[i-1] < lower_barrier and my_time_series['RSI'].iloc[i-2] > lower_barrier:
    my_time_series.at[my_time_series.index[i+1], 'bullish_signal'] = 1
  # bearish signal
  elif my_time_series['RSI'].iloc[i] < upper_barrier and my_time_series['RSI'].iloc[i] > 50 and \
    my_time_series['RSI'].iloc[i-1] > upper_barrier and my_time_series['RSI'].iloc[i-2] < upper_barrier:
    my_time_series.at[my_time_series.index[i+1], 'bearish_signal'] = 1
return my_time_series
```

Figure 3.16 shows a few signals generated by the technique.

Figure 3.16 V technique using RSI

The Double Conservative Confirmation Technique

The second technique is the double conservative confirmation technique (DCC). A personal favorite of mine, despite having significantly less frequency than other techniques, the DCC tends to trigger signals at the end of a major trend. It relies on two RSIs with different lookback periods, coinciding in their conservative signal. The conditions are as follows:

- A bullish signal is generated whenever the 13-period and 34-period RSIs cross over 30.
- A bearish signal is generated whenever the 13-period and 34-period RSIs cross below 70.

The choice of 13 and 34 as lookback periods represents Fibonacci numbers, a concept you will see in detail in Chapter 5. Use the following code to implement the DCC in Python.

```
def rsi_dcc_technique(my_time_series):
  my_time_series = rsi(my_time_series, 'close', 'first_RSI', rsi_lookback=13)
  my_time_series = rsi(my_time_series, 'close', 'second_RSI', rsi_lookback=34)
  my_time_series['bullish_signal'] = 0
  my_time_series['bearish_signal'] = 0
  for i in range(0, len(my_time_series)):
    # bullish signal
    if my_time_series['first_RSI'].iloc[i] > 30 and \
      my_time_series['first_RSI'].iloc[i-1] < 30 and \
      my_time_series['second_RSI'].iloc[i] > 30 and \
      my_time_series['second_RSI'].iloc[i-1] < 30:
      my_time_series.at[my_time_series.index[i+1], 'bullish_signal'] = 1
    # bearish signal
    elif my_time_series['first_RSI'].iloc[i] < 70 and \
      my_time_series['first_RSI'].iloc[i-1] > 70 and \
      my_time_series['second_RSI'].iloc[i] < 70 and \
      my_time_series['second_RSI'].iloc[i-1] > 70:
      my_time_series.at[my_time_series.index[i+1], 'bearish_signal'] = 1
  return my_time_series
```

Figure 3.17 shows a few signals generated by the DCC technique.

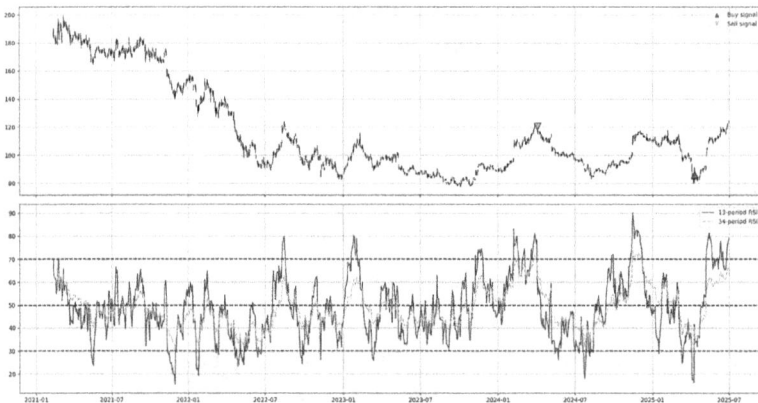

Figure 3.17 DCC technique using RSI

The Moving Average Cross Technique

The third technique is the moving average cross. It entails calculating an SMA on the RSI and using crosses between the two as trading signals. The trading rules of the moving average cross technique are as follows:

- A bullish signal is generated whenever the RSI crosses over its signal line while being below 25.
- A bearish signal is generated whenever the RSI crosses below its signal line while being above 75.

The following code shows how to implement the moving average cross technique.

```python
def rsi_cross_technique(my_time_series, column='close', output_name='RSI', rsi_lookback=5,
lower_barrier=25, upper_barrier=75):
    my_time_series = rsi(my_time_series, column, output_name, rsi_lookback=rsi_lookback)
    my_time_series = moving_average(my_time_series, source='RSI', ma_lookback=5,
output_name='moving_average', ma_type='SMA')
    my_time_series['bullish_signal'] = 0
    my_time_series['bearish_signal'] = 0
    for i in range(0, len(my_time_series)):
        # bullish signal
        if my_time_series['RSI'].iloc[i] > my_time_series['moving_average'].iloc[i] and \
           my_time_series['RSI'].iloc[i-1] < my_time_series['moving_average'].iloc[i-1] and \
           my_time_series['RSI'].iloc[i] < lower_barrier:
            my_time_series.at[my_time_series.index[i+1], 'bullish_signal'] = 1
        # bearish signal
        elif my_time_series['RSI'].iloc[i] < my_time_series['moving_average'].iloc[i] and \
             my_time_series['RSI'].iloc[i-1] > my_time_series['moving_average'].iloc[i-1] and \
             my_time_series['RSI'].iloc[i] > upper_barrier:
            my_time_series.at[my_time_series.index[i+1], 'bearish_signal'] = 1
    return my_time_series
```

Figure 3.18 shows a few signals generated by the moving average cross technique.

Figure 3.18 Moving average cross technique using RSI

In conclusion to this section, you have seen a number of techniques that can enhance the way you interpret the RSI. Additionally, you can create different strategies based on these techniques and back-test them in order to choose the one that suits you.

The Rainbow Indicators

The rainbow collection is a set of seven modern technical indicators that I have developed to provide an uncorrelated opinion on the different market reactions. It is important to set the expectations before diving right into using these indicators. First of all, the concept of an indicator working or not is flawed, as they are not created with the purpose of providing positive returns across all markets and through all time horizons. A technical indicator is nothing but a brick that needs to be put into a fragile wall to solidify it. This means that a signal from an indicator is never enough to create a trade. Then, how should you use these indicators (or any indicator out there)? And what is the added value from using them? The answer to the first question is to consider that their signals are purely price-derived and therefore, they use the past outcomes to signal a future outcome. This adds a certain randomness to the future, which means that you are unlikely to have the same results every time since markets are impacted by a lot of different variables. When you see a signal from an indicator, it generally means that you have to combine it with other signals to form a view. Similarly, it is also better to make sure that the current market regime confirms the signal. The answer to the second question is that they provide a directional added value, but not a trading added value, as they do not tell you where to stop or where to target.

The Red Indicator

The first indicator in the rainbow collection is the Red indicator. I have created this indicator as a fusion between the concept of extreme duration and volatility bands with the aim of detecting the process of returning to normality as early as possible. The concept of extreme duration is a technique I use that imposes a minimum number of time periods outside of the lower/upper boundaries to consider the return to normality as a trading signal (in other words, a confirmed reversal). Hence, by applying the concept of extreme duration on Bollinger bands, you are imposing a minimum number of periods that the market must spend outside of normality (therefore, lower than the lower band or higher than the upper band) before considering the reintegration as a valid signal. The Red indicator calculates Bollinger bands with a small tweak: instead of SMA, EMA is used as the building block. The reason for choosing the EMA is to reduce lag since it gives more weight to the more recent values. Remember, the aim of the Red indicator is to minimize the lag time for the return to normality. The return to normality in terms of Bollinger bands is when the market reaches or breaches one of the bands but then comes back inside them. The exact conditions for the signals are as follows:

- A bullish signal is generated whenever the close price surpasses the lower exponential band after having spent at least five periods below it.
- A bearish signal is generated whenever the close price breaks the upper exponential band after having spent at least five periods above it.

The following code snippet shows the function of the Red indicator.

```
def red_indicator(my_time_series):
  my_time_series = e_bollinger_bands(my_time_series)
  my_time_series['bullish_signal'] = 0
  my_time_series['bearish_signal'] = 0
  for i in range(0, len(my_time_series)):
    # bullish signal
    if my_time_series['close'].iloc[i] < my_time_series['middle_band'].iloc[i] and \
      my_time_series['close'].iloc[i] > my_time_series['lower_band'].iloc[i] and \
      my_time_series['close'].iloc[i-1] < my_time_series['lower_band'].iloc[i-1] and \
      my_time_series['close'].iloc[i-2] < my_time_series['lower_band'].iloc[i-2] and \
      my_time_series['close'].iloc[i-3] < my_time_series['lower_band'].iloc[i-3]:
      my_time_series.at[my_time_series.index[i+1], 'bullish_signal'] = 1
    # bearish signal
    elif my_time_series['close'].iloc[i] > my_time_series['middle_band'].iloc[i] and \
      my_time_series['close'].iloc[i] < my_time_series['upper_band'].iloc[i] and \
      my_time_series['close'].iloc[i-1] > my_time_series['upper_band'].iloc[i-1] and \
      my_time_series['close'].iloc[i-2] > my_time_series['upper_band'].iloc[i-2] and \
      my_time_series['close'].iloc[i-3] > my_time_series['upper_band'].iloc[i-3]:
      my_time_series.at[my_time_series.index[i+1], 'bearish_signal'] = 1
  return my_time_series
```

Figure 3.19 shows the Red indicator in action.

Figure 3.19 The Red indicator

The Red indicator generally gives fewer false signals than other comparable indicators, but it is important to keep in mind the trend-friendly technique of viewing trading signals. One thing to keep in mind is that a return to normality can be done in one candlestick that is so big that there is no more potential left (think of a bearish candlestick that reintegrates the upper Bollinger band and closes around the lower band). Therefore, an optimization method can be applied to the Red indicator, which is to impose a condition that when the current close price surpasses (breaks) the lower (upper) exponential Bollinger band, it must not touch the 20-period EMA. This ensures that there is still potential left. Naturally, one would target the moving average as a first level, but the Red indicator does not really have a rule of thumb when it comes to targets. Keep in mind that there is no such thing as a perfect indicator; all indicators are price-derived or volume-derived, and therefore, an inherent lag is always present. However, on the brighter side, you should not take this as a negative affirmation, as most of the time, what you need to predict the future is the past, since data is the new gold in this era. As a volatility bands' transformation, the Red indicator takes advantage of abnormal periods and tries to forecast the return to normality with minimal lag.

The Orange Indicator

The second indicator in the rainbow collection is the Orange indicator. I have created this indicator out of the pure concept of extreme duration.

The Orange indicator calculates an RSI on the market price and applies a concept referred to as extreme duration to it. The exact conditions for the signals are as follows:

- A bullish signal is generated whenever the current 8-period RSI surpasses 35 but does not go beyond 50, with the next market low reaching below the current open. Additionally, at least the last five RSI values must be below 35.
- A bearish signal is generated whenever the current 8-period RSI breaks 65 but does not go below 50, with the next market high reaching above the current open. Additionally, at least the last five RSI values must be above 65.

The Orange indicator has generally fewer signals than the Red indicator and you must consider the trend in order to maximize its signals, since a low-period RSI can, from time to time, give false signals when the trend is too strong. It is also important to know that the RSI used in the Orange indicator has a low lookback period, and hence, the reactions are expected to be limited. A reasonable way of setting targets is to suppose that the target is reached whenever the RSI hits the other barrier (oversold or overbought level). The following code snippet shows the function of the Orange indicator.

```
def orange_indicator(my_time_series, column='close', output_name='RSI', rsi_lookback=8,
            lower_barrier=35, upper_barrier=65):
  my_time_series = rsi(my_time_series, column, output_name, rsi_lookback=rsi_lookback)
  my_time_series['bullish_signal'] = 0
  my_time_series['bearish_signal'] = 0
  for i in range(0, len(my_time_series)):
    # bullish signal
    if my_time_series['RSI'].iloc[i] > lower_barrier and \
      my_time_series['RSI'].iloc[i] < 50 and \
      my_time_series['RSI'].iloc[i-1] < lower_barrier and \x
      my_time_series['RSI'].iloc[i-2] < lower_barrier and \
      my_time_series['RSI'].iloc[i-3] < lower_barrier and \
      my_time_series['RSI'].iloc[i-4] < lower_barrier and \
      my_time_series['RSI'].iloc[i-5] < lower_barrier:
        my_time_series.at[my_time_series.index[i+1], 'bullish_signal'] = 1
    # bearish signal
    elif my_time_series['RSI'].iloc[i] < upper_barrier and \
      my_time_series['RSI'].iloc[i] > 50 and \
      my_time_series['RSI'].iloc[i-1] > upper_barrier and \
```

```
  my_time_series['RSI'].iloc[i-2] > upper_barrier and\
  my_time_series['RSI'].iloc[i-3] > upper_barrier and\
  my_time_series['RSI'].iloc[i-4] > upper_barrier and\
  my_time_series['RSI'].iloc[i-5] > upper_barrier:
  my_time_series.at[my_time_series.index[i+1], 'bearish_signal'] = 1
return my_time_series
```

Historically, the best results came in flat/ranging markets since supply and demand forces are in an implied equilibrium, which gives the signals equal probabilities.

Figure 3.20 shows the Orange indicator in action.

Figure 3.20 The Orange indicator

The Yellow Indicator

This indicator deals with the concept of slopes as a catalyst for a reversal through divergences. The Yellow indicator detects stagnation in a trend by comparing the slope of the market to the slope of its RSI. Mathematically speaking, the slope is a measure of the steepness of a line. It describes how much a line (price or value of a technical indicator) rises or falls as it moves chronologically. The slope is defined as the ratio of the change in price with regard to time. The slope is defined as the ratio of the change in the *y*-coordinate (vertical) to the change in the *x*-coordinate (horizontal) between any two points on the line. It is also called the gradient. The slope formula is as follows:

$$\text{Slope} = \frac{y_i - y_{i-n}}{x_i - x_{i-n}}$$

The slope can be positive, negative, zero, or undefined, depending on the direction and steepness of the line. A positive slope indicates that the line is sloping upward from left to right, while a negative slope indicates that the line is sloping downward from left to right. A slope of zero indicates that the line is horizontal, while an undefined slope indicates that the line is vertical.

If there's a divergence in the slope, then a signal is generated as shown below:

- A bullish signal is generated whenever the current 14-period RSI slope moves above zero while the current and previous 14-period market slope are below zero. Additionally, the most recent RSI reading must be below 35.
- A bearish signal is generated whenever the current 14-period RSI slope moves below zero while the current and previous 14-period market slope are above zero. Additionally, the most recent RSI reading must be above 65.

The following code snippet shows the function of the Yellow indicator.

```python
def yellow_indicator(my_time_series, column='close', output_name='RSI', lower_barrier=35,
                     upper_barrier=65):
    my_time_series = rsi(my_time_series, column, output_name, rsi_lookback=14)
    my_time_series = slope(my_time_series, source='RSI', output_name='slope_rsi',
                           slope_lookback=14)
    my_time_series = slope(my_time_series, source='close', output_name='slope_market',
                           slope_lookback=14)
    my_time_series['bullish_signal'] = 0
    my_time_series['bearish_signal'] = 0
    for i in range(0, len(my_time_series)):
        # bullish signal
        if my_time_series['slope_rsi'].iloc[i] > 0 and \
          my_time_series['slope_rsi'].iloc[i-1] < 0 and \
          my_time_series['slope_market'].iloc[i] < 0 and \
          my_time_series['slope_market'].iloc[i-1] < 0 and \
          my_time_series['RSI'].iloc[i] < lower_barrier:
            my_time_series.at[my_time_series.index[i+1], 'bullish_signal'] = 1
        # bearish signal
        elif my_time_series['slope_rsi'].iloc[i] < 0 and \
          my_time_series['slope_rsi'].iloc[i-1] > 0 and \
          my_time_series['slope_market'].iloc[i] > 0 and \
          my_time_series['slope_market'].iloc[i-1] > 0 and \
          my_time_series['RSI'].iloc[i] > upper_barrier:
            my_time_series.at[my_time_series.index[i+1], 'bearish_signal'] = 1
    return my_time_series
```

Figure 3.21 shows the Yellow indicator in action.

Figure 3.21 The Yellow indicator

The Green Indicator

The fourth indicator in the rainbow collection is the Green indicator. Occasionally, markets' slopes tend to flatten before reversing. The Green indicator calculates a 13-period RSI and then calculates a 5-period slope on the RSI. It therefore measures the slope of the RSI with respect to its value five periods ago at every time step. The exact conditions for the signals are as follows:

- A bullish signal is generated whenever the current 14-period slope on the 14-period RSI surpasses zero while the 14-period RSI is below 35.
- A bearish signal is generated whenever the current 14-period slope on the 14-period RSI breaks zero while the 14-period RSI is above 65.

Preferably, the Green indicator must be used in a ranging market as it tends to underperform during a healthy trending market. Depending on the slope, the Green indicator may give interesting opportunities for a reaction (generally short-term). The following code snippet shows the function of the Green indicator.

```
def green_indicator(my_time_series, column='close', output_name='RSI',
rsi_lookback=14,
              slope_lookback=14, lower_barrier=35, upper_barrier=65):
  my_time_series = rsi(my_time_series, source='close', output_name='RSI',
              rsi_lookback=rsi_lookback)
  my_time_series = slope(my_time_series, source='RSI',
output_name='slope',
              slope_lookback=slope_lookback)
  my_time_series['bullish_signal'] = 0
  my_time_series['bearish_signal'] = 0
  for i in range(0, len(my_time_series)):
    # bullish signal
    if my_time_series['slope'].iloc[i] > 0 and \
      my_time_series['slope'].iloc[i-1] < 0 and \
      my_time_series['RSI'].iloc[i] < lower_barrier:
      my_time_series.at[my_time_series.index[i+1], 'bullish_signal'] = 1
    # bearish signal
    elif my_time_series['slope'].iloc[i] < 0 and \
      my_time_series['slope'].iloc[i-1] > 0 and \
      my_time_series['RSI'].iloc[i] > upper_barrier:
      my_time_series.at[my_time_series.index[i+1], 'bearish_signal'] = 1
  return my_time_series
```

Figure 3.22 shows the Green indicator in action.

Figure 3.22 The Green indicator

To sum up, the Green indicator searches for signals by using the concept of slopes applied to the RSI while it is deep in the overbought or oversold zone.

The Blue Indicator

The Blue indicator shares a few similarities with the Green indicator as it makes use of the slope concept and the RSI. The slope function is applied to the closing price, then the RSI is applied to the slope calculation from before. The exact conditions for the signals are as follows:

- A bullish signal is generated whenever the current RSI slope calculation crosses over 30 but remains below 35. Simultaneously, the low price must be below the low from the previous period.
- A bearish signal is generated whenever the current RSI slope calculation crosses under 70 but remains above 65. Simultaneously, the high price must be above the high from the previous period.

The following code snippet shows the function of the Blue indicator.

```
def blue_indicator(my_time_series, column='close', output_name='RSI', rsi_lookback=5,
        slope_lookback=5, lower_barrier=30, upper_barrier=70, margin=5):
    my_time_series = slope(my_time_series, source='close', output_name='slope',
            slope_lookback=slope_lookback)
    my_time_series = rsi(my_time_series, source='slope', output_name='RSI_slope',
            rsi_lookback=rsi_lookback)
    my_time_series['bullish_signal'] = 0
    my_time_series['bearish_signal'] = 0
    for i in range(0, len(my_time_series)):
        # bullish signal
        if my_time_series['RSI_slope'].iloc[i] > lower_barrier and \
        my_time_series['RSI_slope'].iloc[i] < lower_barrier + margin and \
        my_time_series['RSI_slope'].iloc[i-1] < lower_barrier and \
        my_time_series['low'].iloc[i] < my_time_series['low'].iloc[i-1]:
            my_time_series.at[my_time_series.index[i+1], 'bullish_signal'] = 1
        # bearish signal
        elif my_time_series['RSI_slope'].iloc[i] < upper_barrier and \
        my_time_series['RSI_slope'].iloc[i] > upper_barrier - margin and \
        my_time_series['RSI_slope'].iloc[i-1] > upper_barrier and \
        my_time_series['high'].iloc[i] > my_time_series['high'].iloc[i-1]:
            my_time_series.at[my_time_series.index[i+1], 'bearish_signal'] = 1
    return my_time_series
```

Figure 3.23 shows the Blue indicator in action.

Figure 3.23 The Blue indicator

The Indigo Indicator

The sixth indicator in the rainbow collection is the Indigo indicator. This indicator may be considered a pattern recognition tool with fixed conditions. The exact conditions for the signals are as follows:

- A bullish signal is generated whenever the current close price crosses over the previous close price while the close prices from {1, 2, 3, 5, 8, 13, 21} periods ago are below the close prices from {2, 3, 5, 8, 13, 21, 34} periods ago, respectively.
- A bearish signal is generated whenever the current close price crosses under the previous close price while the close prices from {1, 2, 3, 5, 8, 13, 21} periods ago are above the close prices from {2, 3, 5, 8, 13, 21, 34} periods ago, respectively.

The following code snippet shows the function of the Indigo indicator.

```
def indigo_indicator(my_time_series, source='close'):
  my_time_series['bullish_signal'] = 0
  my_time_series['bearish_signal'] = 0
  for i in range(0, len(my_time_series)):
    # bullish signal
    if my_time_series[source].iloc[i] > my_time_series[source].iloc[i-1] and \
      my_time_series[source].iloc[i-1] < my_time_series[source].iloc[i-2] and \
      my_time_series[source].iloc[i-2] < my_time_series[source].iloc[i-3] and \
      my_time_series[source].iloc[i-3] < my_time_series[source].iloc[i-5] and \
      my_time_series[source].iloc[i-5] < my_time_series[source].iloc[i-8] and \
      my_time_series[source].iloc[i-8] < my_time_series[source].iloc[i-13] and \
```

```
        my_time_series[source].iloc[i-13] < my_time_series[source].iloc[i-21] and \
        my_time_series[source].iloc[i-21] < my_time_series[source].iloc[i-34]:
        my_time_series.at[my_time_series.index[i+1], 'bullish_signal'] = 1
    # bearish signal
    elif my_time_series[source].iloc[i] < my_time_series[source].iloc[i-1] and \
        my_time_series[source].iloc[i-1] > my_time_series[source].iloc[i-2] and \
        my_time_series[source].iloc[i-2] > my_time_series[source].iloc[i-3] and \
        my_time_series[source].iloc[i-3] > my_time_series[source].iloc[i-5] and \
        my_time_series[source].iloc[i-5] > my_time_series[source].iloc[i-8] and \
        my_time_series[source].iloc[i-8] > my_time_series[source].iloc[i-13] and \
        my_time_series[source].iloc[i-13] > my_time_series[source].iloc[i-21] and \
        my_time_series[source].iloc[i-21] > my_time_series[source].iloc[i-34]:
        my_time_series.at[my_time_series.index[i+1], 'bearish_signal'] = 1
return my_time_series
```

Figure 3.24 shows the Indigo indicator in action.

Figure 3.24 The Indigo indicator

The Violet Indicator

Lastly, the seventh indicator in the rainbow collection is the Violet indicator. This indicator uses the HMA and the Fibonacci sequence (similar to the Indigo indicator). The exact conditions for the signals are as follows:

- A bullish signal is generated when the current closing price crosses above the HMA, while the closing prices from the previous Fibonacci lookbacks — {1, 2, 3, 5, 8, 13, 21} periods ago — were all below their corresponding HMA values.
- A bearish signal is generated when the current closing price crosses below the HMA, while the closing prices from {1, 2, 3, 5, 8, 13, 21} periods ago were all above their corresponding HMA values.

The following code snippet shows the function of the Violet indicator.

```python
def violet_indicator(my_time_series, source='close', ma_source='HMA'):
  my_time_series = hma(my_time_series, ma_lookback=20)
  my_time_series['bullish_signal'] = 0
  my_time_series['bearish_signal'] = 0
  for i in range(0, len(my_time_series)):
    # bullish signal
    if my_time_series[source].iloc[i] > my_time_series[ma_source].iloc[i] and \
      my_time_series[source].iloc[i-1] < my_time_series[ma_source].iloc[i-1] and \
      my_time_series[source].iloc[i-2] < my_time_series[ma_source].iloc[i-2] and \
      my_time_series[source].iloc[i-3] < my_time_series[ma_source].iloc[i-3] and \
      my_time_series[source].iloc[i-5] < my_time_series[ma_source].iloc[i-5] and \
      my_time_series[source].iloc[i-8] < my_time_series[ma_source].iloc[i-8] and \
      my_time_series[source].iloc[i-13] < my_time_series[ma_source].iloc[i-13] and \
      my_time_series[source].iloc[i-21] < my_time_series[ma_source].iloc[i-21]:
      my_time_series.at[my_time_series.index[i+1], 'bullish_signal'] = 1
    # bearish signal
    elif my_time_series[source].iloc[i] < my_time_series[ma_source].iloc[i] and \
      my_time_series[source].iloc[i-1] > my_time_series[ma_source].iloc[i-1] and \
      my_time_series[source].iloc[i-2] > my_time_series[ma_source].iloc[i-2] and \
      my_time_series[source].iloc[i-3] > my_time_series[ma_source].iloc[i-3] and \
      my_time_series[source].iloc[i-5] > my_time_series[ma_source].iloc[i-5] and \
      my_time_series[source].iloc[i-8] > my_time_series[ma_source].iloc[i-8] and \
      my_time_series[source].iloc[i-13] > my_time_series[ma_source].iloc[i-13] and \
      my_time_series[source].iloc[i-21] > my_time_series[ma_source].iloc[i-21]:
      my_time_series.at[my_time_series.index[i+1], 'bearish_signal'] = 1
  return my_time_series
```

Figure 3.25 shows the Violet indicator in action.

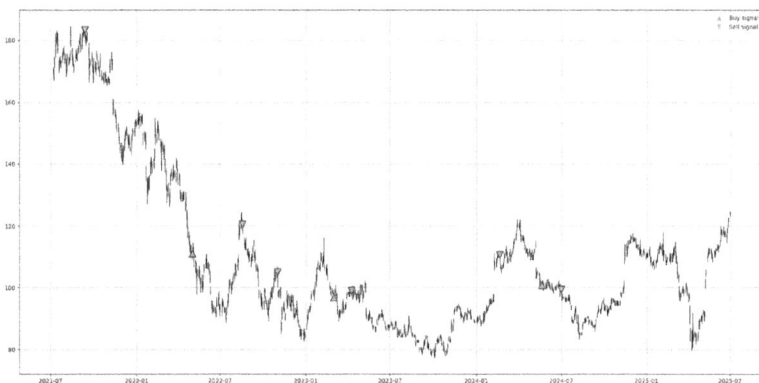

Figure 3.25 The Violet indicator

The Violet indicator is an indicator that deals with moving average cross techniques. It means that it detects the change in trend whenever there is an event related to the close price and the moving average. To sum up, the Violet indicator takes into consideration the HMA that tries to reduce lag and applies a technique on it that signals early reversals. This indicator may have more signals than other indicators, and therefore, it may provide more opportunities. The rainbow indicators are not supposed to be perfect indicators. In fact, they vary from one period to another in performance, just like any other indicator out there. The best way to use the rainbow indicators is to combine them together and see whether there are signals that occur around the same time period or not. Ideally, they should occur around ±3 time periods from each other for a signal to be strong. You can also combine the rainbow indicators with classic indicators such as the RSI. Make sure you back-test your ideas before making any assumptions.

CHAPTER 4

Alternative Charting Systems

Charts are your first line of offense with technical analysis. The visual interpretation part is extremely crucial in determining first impressions. This chapter will serve to introduce alternative charting systems that you can use to improve market interpretations.

Volume Candlesticks Charting System

Volume candlesticks require volume data. They get bigger the more volume there is. This means that small (width-wise and not length-wise) candlesticks will represent low volume, while big candlesticks will represent bigger volume. Therefore, volume candlesticks can give a quick snapshot of the current volume health, which may indirectly help to determine the health of the trend. As you may have probably noticed, this type of charting system requires quality volume data; therefore, it would be complicated to use with decentralized markets such as the FX market. On the other hand, stock markets are better-suited for this type of charting. Figure 4.1 shows a theoretical illustration of a volume candlestick charting system.

Imagine noticing a breakout candlestick on a standard candlestick chart—it looks bullish. But on a volume candlestick chart, you notice low volume behind it. That's a red flag, as it could be a fake breakout. This is the main advantage of this type of chart. In markets where volume fluctuates a lot, volume candles help you filter noise and only focus on candles that truly matter. The following code snippet shows how to create this charting system.

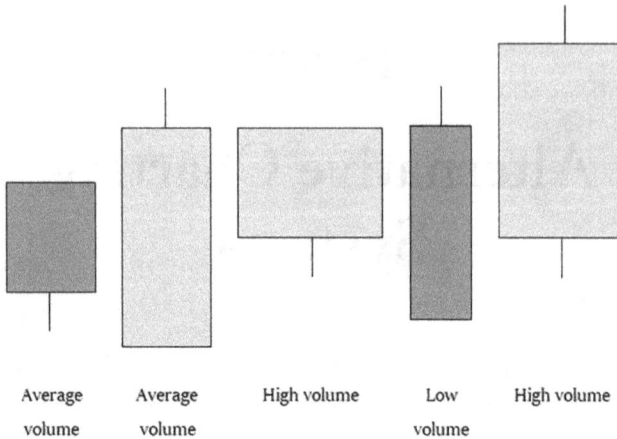

| Average volume | Average volume | High volume | Low volume | High volume |

Figure 4.1 Volume candlesticks

```
def volume_candlestick_plot(my_time_series, window=250):
    sample = my_time_series.iloc[-window:, ]
    fig, ax = plt.subplots(figsize = (10, 5))
    for i in sample.index:
        plt.vlines(x = i, ymin = sample.at[i, 'low'], ymax = sample.at[i, 'high'], color = 'black', linewidth = 1)
        if sample.at[i, 'close'] > sample.at[i, 'open'] and sample.at[i, 'normalized'] >= 0.75:
            plt.vlines(x = i, ymin = sample.at[i, 'open'], ymax = sample.at[i, 'close'], color = 'green', linewidth = 7)
        elif sample.at[i, 'close'] > sample.at[i, 'open'] and sample.at[i, 'normalized'] < 0.75 and sample.at[i,
                                    'normalized'] >= 0.50:
            plt.vlines(x = i, ymin = sample.at[i, 'open'], ymax = sample.at[i, 'close'], color = 'green', linewidth = 5)
        elif sample.at[i, 'close'] > sample.at[i, 'open'] and sample.at[i, 'normalized'] > 0.25 and sample.at[i,
        'normalized'] < 0.50:
            plt.vlines(x = i, ymin = sample.at[i, 'open'], ymax = sample.at[i, 'close'], color = 'green', linewidth = 3)
        elif sample.at[i, 'close'] > sample.at[i, 'open'] and sample.at[i, 'normalized'] <= 0.25:
            plt.vlines(x = i, ymin = sample.at[i, 'open'], ymax = sample.at[i, 'close'], color = 'green', linewidth = 2)
        elif sample.at[i, 'close'] < sample.at[i, 'open'] and sample.at[i, 'normalized'] >= 0.75:
            plt.vlines(x = i, ymin = sample.at[i, 'close'], ymax = sample.at[i, 'open'], color = 'red', linewidth = 7)
        elif sample.at[i, 'close'] < sample.at[i, 'open'] and sample.at[i, 'normalized'] >= 0.50:
            plt.vlines(x = i, ymin = sample.at[i, 'close'], ymax = sample.at[i, 'open'], color = 'red', linewidth = 5)
        elif sample.at[i, 'close'] < sample.at[i, 'open'] and sample.at[i, 'normalized'] > 0.25 and sample.at[i,
        'normalized'] < 0.50:
            plt.vlines(x = i, ymin = sample.at[i, 'close'], ymax = sample.at[i, 'open'], color = 'red', linewidth = 3)
        elif sample.at[i, 'close'] < sample.at[i, 'open'] and sample.at[i, 'normalized'] <= 0.25:
            plt.vlines(x = i, ymin = sample.at[i, 'close'], ymax = sample.at[i, 'open'], color = 'red', linewidth = 2)
        elif sample.at[i, 'close'] == sample.at[i, 'open']:
            plt.vlines(x = i, ymin = sample.at[i, 'close'], ymax = sample.at[i, 'open'], color = 'black', linewidth = 1)
    plt.grid()
    plt.show()
    plt.tight_layout()
```

Figure 4.2 shows the output of the code.

Figure 4.2 A chart showing volume candlesticks

Heikin-Ashi System

Heikin-Ashi is a type of candlestick chart used to filter out market noise and provide a clearer picture of the trend. Heikin-Ashi candles are calculated differently from traditional candlesticks. The Heikin-Ashi close price is calculated as the average of the current session's OHLC average:

$$Heikin_{close} = \frac{(Open + high + low + close)}{4}$$

The Heikin-Ashi open price is calculated as the average between the last open and close prices:

$$Heikin_{open} = \frac{(Heikin_{open_{i-1}} + Heikin_{close_{i-1}})}{2}$$

The Heikin-Ashi high price is calculated as the maximum value between the following:

$$Heikin_{high} = max(High, Heikin_{open}, Heikin_{close})$$

The Heikin-Ashi low price is calculated as the minimum value between the following:

$$Heikin_{low} = min(Low, Heikin_{open}, Heikin_{close})$$

Let's see the characteristics of this powerful charting system:

• During a bullish trend, you typically see a series of consecutive bullish candles. The candles usually have no lower shadows. This indicates strong bullish momentum.
• During a bearish trend, you typically see a series of consecutive bearish candles. The candles usually have no upper shadows. This indicates strong bearish momentum.

The following function defines the Heikin-Ashi charting system.

```
def heikin_ashi(my_time_series):
  # close price using heikin-ashi
  my_time_series['HA_close'] = (my_time_series['open'] + my_time_series['high'] + my_time_se-
ries['low'] + my_time_series['close']) / 4
  # open price using heikin-ashi
  my_time_series['HA_open'] = 0
  my_time_series['HA_open'].iloc[0] = my_time_series['open'].iloc[0]
  for i in range(1, len(my_time_series)):
    my_time_series.at[my_time_series.index[i], 'HA_open'] = (my_time_series['HA_open'].iloc[i-1] + \
                            my_time_series['HA_close'].iloc[i-1]) / 2
  # high price using heikin-ashi
  my_time_series['HA_high'] = my_time_series[['high', 'HA_open', 'HA_close']].max(axis=1)
  # low price using heikin-ashi
  my_time_series['HA_low'] = my_time_series[['low', 'HA_open', 'HA_close']].min(axis=1)
  return my_time_series.dropna()
```

Figure 4.3 shows the difference between a standard candlestick chart and a Heikin-Ashi chart. Notice how the latter renders the data smooth for a better interpretation.

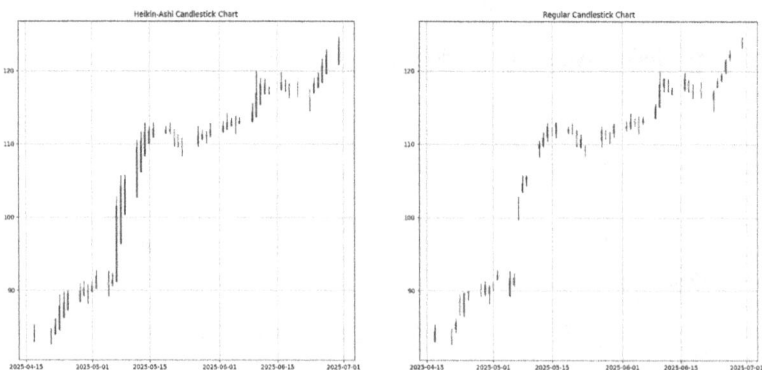

Figure 4.3 Heikin-Ashi candlesticks (left). *Regular candlesticks* (right)

Heikin-Ashi candles use averaged data, so trends appear smoother. It filters out short-term volatility and meaningless wicks, which can be helpful in choppy markets, where normal candlesticks can mislead.

K's Candlestick Charting System

This charting system is inspired by Heikin-Ashi charts. Its main aim is to smooth the data and improve the efficacy of candlestick patterns (see Chapter 7 for more details on candlestick patterns). Here's how the system calculates the OHLC data:

$$K'sCCS_{close} = \frac{(Close_i + close_{i-1} + close_{i-2} + close_{i-3} + close_{i-4})}{5}$$

The K's candlestick charting system (CCS) open price is calculated as the average of the previous five open prices:

$$K'sCCS_{open} = \frac{(Open_i + open_{i-1} + open_{i-2} + open_{i-3} + open_{i-4})}{5}$$

The K's CCS high price is calculated as the average of the previous five high prices:

$$K'sCCS_{high} = \frac{(High_i + high_{i-1} + high_{i-2} + high_{i-3} + high_{i-4})}{5}$$

The K's CCS low price is calculated as the average of the previous five low prices:

$$K'sCCS_{low} = \frac{(Low_i + low_{i-1} + low_{i-2} + low_{i-3} + low_{i-4})}{5}$$

Use the following function to create K's CCS.

```
def k_candlesticks(my_time_series, k_lookback=5):
    # calculating the exponential moving average on the ohlc data
```

```
my_time_series = moving_average(my_time_series, 'open',
ma_lookback=k_lookback,
                    output_name='k_open', ma_type='EMA')
my_time_series = moving_average(my_time_series, 'high',
ma_lookback=k_lookback,
    output_name='k_high', ma_type='EMA')
my_time_series = moving_average(my_time_series, 'low',
ma_lookback=k_lookback,
     output_name='k_low',  ma_type='EMA')
my_time_series = moving_average(my_time_series, 'close',
ma_lookback=k_lookback,
        output_name='k_close', ma_type='EMA')
return my_time_series.dropna()
```

Figure 4.4 shows K's CCS in action. You can notice how smooth the chart is. However, as it's a 5-period average of OHLC data, it has a slight lag in it.

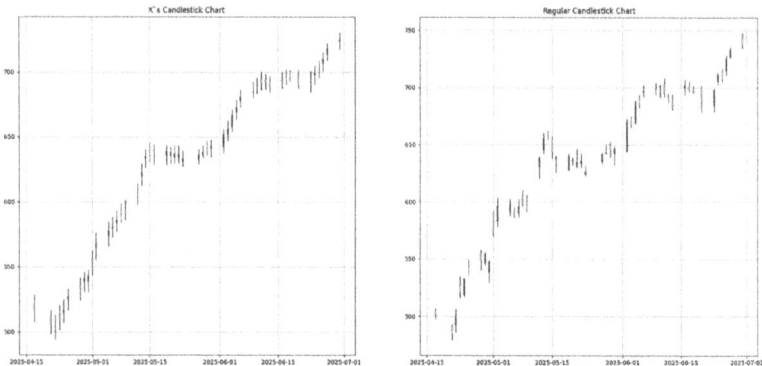

Figure 4.4 K's candlesticks (left). *Regular candlesticks* (right)

Remember that in this book, we often use a custom Python library called **master_library**, which contains many of the functions that you will see across the chapters. To keep the code clean and organized, we place related functions into this single file and import only what we need in each program. If you only need certain functions (e.g., **moving_average** and **generate_ohlc_data**), you can import them like this:

```
from master_library import moving_average, generate_ohlc_data
```

The Candlestick RSI

The candlestick RSI (CARSI) is simply an OHLC-based RSI, and therefore, can be a proxy of normalized OHLC data that hovers from 0 to 100. Let's see the steps needed to create CARSI:

1. Apply the RSI formula on the open, high, low, and close prices:

$$RSI_{open} = RSI(open, 14)$$
$$RSI_{high} = RSI(high, 14)$$
$$RSI_{low} = RSI(low, 14)$$
$$RSI_{close} = RSI(close, 14)$$

2. To find the real candlestick RSI open price, apply this formula:

$$Open_{RSI} = min(RSI_{open}, RSI_{close}) \text{ if open} < \text{close}$$
$$Open_{RSI} = max(RSI_{open}, RSI_{close}) \text{ if open} > \text{close}$$

3. To find the real candlestick RSI high price, apply this formula:

$$High_{RSI} = max(RSI_{open}, RSI_{high}, RSI_{low}, RSI_{close})$$

4. To find the real candlestick RSI low price, apply this formula:

$$Low_{RSI} = min(RSI_{open}, RSI_{high}, RSI_{low}, RSI_{close})$$

5. To find the real candlestick RSI close price, apply this formula:

$$Close_{RSI} = min(RSI_{open}, RSI_{close}) \text{ if open} > \text{close}$$
$$Close_{RSI} = max(RSI_{open}, RSI_{close}) \text{ if open} < \text{close}$$

You can find the code for CARSI in the GitHub repository due to its length. Figure 4.5 shows CARSI in action.[6]

---

[6]GitHub link: https://github.com/sofienkaabar/mastering-financial-markets-in-python

Figure 4.5 **CARSI**

It resembles a normal candlestick chart that seems to be bounded between predetermined levels (in this case, 0 and 100). You can use the chart the same way as you would use the RSI. In Chapter 7, you will learn about CARSI patterns in detail.

CHAPTER 5

Advanced Fibonacci Analysis in Python

Leonardo Bonacci (c. 1170 to c. 1240–1250), sometimes referred to as Fibonacci (as in the son of Bonacci), was an Italian mathematician who worked in the early thirteenth century and is the creator of the Fibonacci sequence. In 1202, he wrote his treatise *Liber Abaci*, which introduced the sequence. In his work, Fibonacci addressed the issue of estimating the expansion of a rabbit population. He asked, "If each couple begets a new pair every month, starting in the second month, how many pairs of rabbits are generated by a single pair in a year?" He developed the sequence that is now known as the Fibonacci sequence to address this issue. Each number in the Fibonacci sequence is formed by adding the two numbers before it. The sequence's first numbers are: 0, 1, 1, 2, 3, 5, 8, 13, 21, 34, 55, and so on. The sequence is infinite, and as the numbers increase exponentially, the ratio of any two successive numbers becomes closer to a certain number referred to as the golden ratio, which is approximately 1.618. This pattern allowed Fibonacci to simulate the expansion of the rabbit population, and he discovered that Fibonacci numbers offer a prediction of the number of pairs of rabbits that would be born after a specific number of months. Since then, a great deal of research has been conducted on the Fibonacci sequence, and it has been discovered to be related to many branches of mathematics as well as nature, art, and architecture. Mathematically speaking, any Fibonacci number is found using the following formula:

$$x_i = x_{i-1} + x_{i-2}$$

The Fibonacci ratios are derived from the Fibonacci sequence, where every number is divided by the number that precedes it (rank-wise). This can be done using the following formula:

$$\varphi_i = \frac{x_i}{x_{i_{-1}}} \rightarrow \infty \approx 1.618$$

This can be demonstrated by the following divisions:

144/89 = 1.617977   233/377 = 1.618025   1597/987 = 1.618034

As the numbers tend toward infinity, the ratio approaches 1.618, and this is why it is referred to as the golden ratio. Note that the golden ratio is represented by the Phi symbol φ. Fibonacci numbers and ratios can be found in biological entities, in music, and in a more disputed way, in weather and astronomy. Fibonacci ratios are derived from the golden ratio. Note that Fibonacci ratios are represented in percentages (hence, the golden ratio 1.618 becomes 161.8%). The ratio 61.8% is what you get when you subtract 1 from 1.618 (conjugate) and when you divide 1 by 1.618 (reciprocal). The list of ratios that you must familiarize yourself with is as follows:

23.6%	Cube of 61.8%	78.6%	Square root of 61.8%	161.8%	Golden ratio
38.2%	Square of 61.8%	88.6%	Cube root of 61.8%	200.0%	Twice the distance
50.0%	Half the distance	100.0%	Full distance	224.0%	61.8% + 161.8%
61.8%	Reciprocal of 161.8%	113.0%	Reciprocal of 88.6%	261.8%	Sum of 1 + 161.8%

Fibonacci Retracements and Projections

A retracement is the act of going back the same route you have already taken. In technical analysis, a retracement is when a market shapes a top or bottom and starts recovering (after a bottom) or correcting (after a top). The main idea of Fibonacci retracements is to find support and resistance levels using certain Fibonacci ratios. Here's what you need to know:

- Support levels are given after a top is shaped and the market starts to correct lower. They are found by calculating the percentage distance of the rise measured from the first bottom (low price) to the newly shaped top (high price).

- Resistance levels are given after a bottom is shaped and the market starts to recover. They are found by calculating the percentage distance of the drop measured from the first top (high price) to the newly shaped bottom (low price).

Fibonacci support levels are retracements of a bullish move, and they give the levels from where the initial bullish move should continue or at least from where a limited bullish reaction is expected. On the other hand, Fibonacci resistance levels are retracements of a bearish move, and they give the levels from where the initial bearish move should continue or at least from where a limited bearish reaction is expected (Figure 5.1).

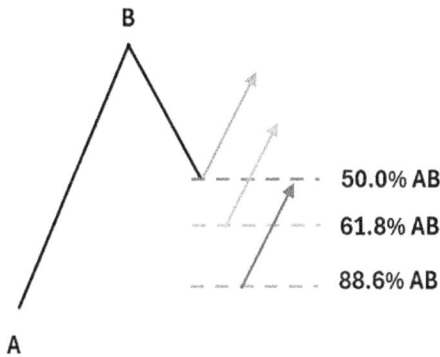

Figure 5.1 Fibonacci retracements

Fibonacci projections extend beyond a current price range to forecast future price movements. These projections help identify potential price targets beyond the current swing high or swing low. To calculate Fibonacci projections, traders typically identify three points on a price chart:

1. A significant low (or high), also known as point A
2. A subsequent high (or low), also known as point B
3. A retracement to a significant low (or high), also known as point C

Projections are made by measuring the price distance between A and B, then extending it forward from C by applying Fibonacci ratios such as

61.8%, 100%, 161.8%, 261.8%, and so on. It is worth noting that 100% is equivalent to the full distance of the price move from A to B (this is also referred to as an ABCD pattern, which you will see in Chapter 8) (Figure 5.2).

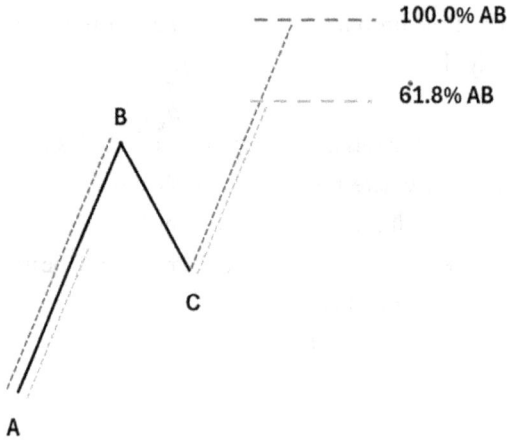

Figure 5.2 Fibonacci extensions

Classic technical analysis makes a few assumptions about certain Fibonacci levels that modern technical analysis transforms into clear, rules-based, and back-testable algorithms. The following two classic assumptions will be coded and visualized:

- Whenever the market retraces back to 23.6% of the initial move and breaks it, a further continuation of the move is likely.
- Whenever the market retraces back to 61.8% of the initial move, a contrarian reaction is expected.

But first, you need to understand what swing points are in order to be able to construct retracement and projection algorithms.

An Important Concept: Swing Highs and Lows

Swing highs and swing lows (both also known as swing points) are fundamental concepts in technical analysis, especially relevant in the context of identifying market structure, trend formation, and potential reversal points. In a time series composed of sequential price observations (e.g., daily closing prices), a swing high is a local maximum that occurs between two lower highs. Conversely, a swing low is a local minimum flanked by two higher lows. Formally, for a discrete time series P_t, where $t \in \{1, 2, ..., t\}$, a swing high at time t satisfies the following statement:

$$P_{t-k} < P_t > P_{t+k}$$

And a swing low at t satisfies:

$$P_{t-k} > P_t < P_{t+k}$$

Here, k represents the lookback or the window size before and after the current point, typically set to a few bars so that the swing is visible and less noisy. For example, a 20-period lookback period can be sufficient to judge the swings. From a time series perspective, swing highs and lows correspond to local extrema—peaks and troughs—that provide insight into the structure of the underlying process generating the prices. These points are not only statistical observations; they also hold significant interpretive value in the study of trend evolution, cyclicality, and mean-reverting behavior. Swing highs and lows serve as structural markers in a time series. A sequence of higher swing highs and higher swing lows characterizes an uptrend, suggesting a directional bias in the underlying stochastic process. Conversely, lower swing highs and lower swing lows define a downtrend, indicating a shift in regime. They allow for the segmentation of a time series into trend-based components, each with its own statistical properties (mean, variance, volatility) (Figure 5.3).

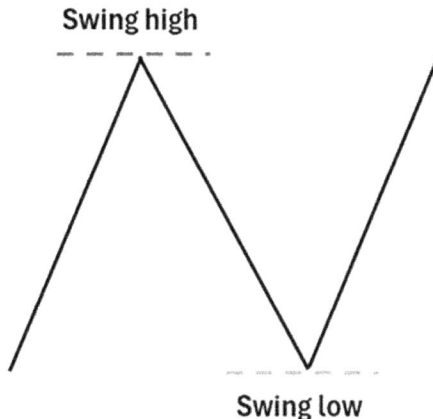

Figure 5.3 A swing high and a swing low

Unlike fixed-interval technical indicators (e.g., moving averages), swing points are event-based rather than time-based. This distinction is crucial in time series analysis because it shifts the focus from the passage of time to the emergence of significant price movements. Swing highs and lows thus provide a nonlinear sampling of the time series— highlighting the most informative moments when the market exhibits behavioral shifts, often tied to liquidity imbalances, institutional activity, or macroeconomic catalysts. From a coding and computational standpoint, swing points are typically detected using a rolling window approach over a time series. Let k be the window size. At each point t, the price is compared with its neighbors:

$$\text{Swing high}: \text{if } P_t = \max(P_{t-k}, ..., P_t, ..., P_{t+k})$$
$$\text{Swing low}: \text{if } P_t = \min(P_{t-k}, ..., P_t, ..., P_{t+k})$$

This method formalizes the process and enables batch detection across large datasets. Let's see how to code them using a simple function that will be used heavily in the coming chapters.

```python
def swing_detect(my_time_series, swing_lookback=20):
    my_time_series['swing_low'] = my_time_series['low'].rolling(window=swing_lookback, min_periods=1,
                                    center=True).min()
    my_time_series['swing_low'] = my_time_series.apply(lambda row: row['low'] if row['low'] ==
                                    row['swing_low'] else 0, axis=1)
    my_time_series['swing_low'] = my_time_series['swing_low'].replace(0, np.nan)
    my_time_series['swing_high'] = my_time_series['high'].rolling(window=swing_lookback,
min_periods=1,
                                    center=True).max()
    my_time_series['swing_high'] = my_time_series.apply(lambda row: row['high'] if row['high'] ==
                                    row['swing_high'] else 0, axis=1)
    my_time_series['swing_high'] = my_time_series['swing_high'].replace(0, np.nan)
    return my_time_series
```

The variable **swing_lookback** controls how strict or sensitive the swing detection is:

- A larger value will find fewer but more significant swing points (more smoothing).
- A smaller value will find more frequent swing points (more sensitive to short-term fluctuations).

Swing points are visible on the chart in Figure 5.4.

Figure 5.4 Swing points (circles) detected on a time series

Swing highs and lows are more than just visual turning points on a price chart—they are fundamental elements of time series structure in financial markets. They capture the essence of how markets move, pause, and reverse, acting as building blocks for trend formation and market cycle analysis. You will now see the first usage of swing highs and lows in Fibonacci retracements.

The 23.6% Reintegration Technique

According to classic technical analysis, breaking the 23.6% retracement level can further accelerate the ongoing move and give credit to a deeper correction in case of an uptrend or to a bigger recovery in case of a downtrend. Here's how:

- During a bullish market with a bottom at point A, if a top is seen at point B and the 23.6% AB retracement is broken down, further downside potential can be expected.
- During a bearish market with a top at point A, if a bottom is seen at point B and the 23.6% AB retracement is surpassed, further upside potential can be expected.

The following illustration shows the assumption visually. The dashed line shows the expected trajectory after the fulfillment of the condition. Generally, the move should extend to 61.8% of the AB retracement after the break (Figure 5.5).

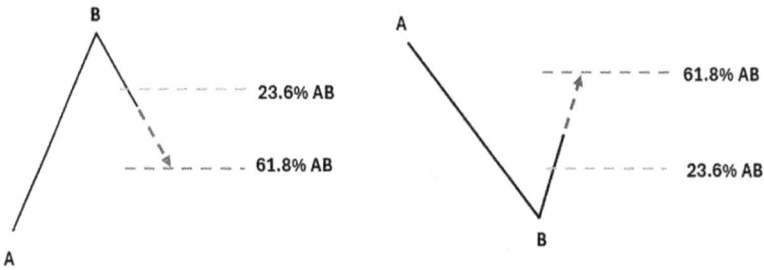

Figure 5.5 A theoretical illustration of the reintegration technique

It's crucial to understand the logic of swing points with what we are trying to do with retracements:

- Consider point A as a swing low and point B as a swing high. Calculating the difference between point A and point B, multiplying it by 0.236, and subtracting the total from point B will give the 23.6% support of AB, which needs to be broken down to confirm a deeper correction. This is known as the 23.6% Fibonacci retracement of the AB point. It can also be referred to as the first Fibonacci support level.
- Consider point A as a swing high and point B as a swing low. Calculating the difference between point A and point B, multiplying it by 0.236, and adding the total to point B will give the 23.6% resistance of AB, which needs to be surpassed to confirm a bigger recovery. This is known as the 23.6% Fibonacci retracement of the AB point. It can also be referred to as the first Fibonacci resistance level.

If classic technical analysis assumes that the break of 23.6% confirms more potential, modern technical analysis codes this assumption and visualizes it through time. This helps us understand its efficacy and further improve and back-test it. Use the following code to create the function that detects Fibonacci retracements (in this case, it detects the 23.6% level as set by the variable fib_level).

```
def fibonacci_retracement(my_time_series, swing_lookback=20, fib_level=0.236):
    my_time_series = swing_detect(my_time_series, swing_lookback=swing_lookback)
    my_time_series['support'] = np.nan
```

```
my_time_series['resistance'] = np.nan
last_swing_type = None
last_swing_value = None
for i, row in my_time_series.iterrows():
  if not np.isnan(row['swing_high']):
    current_type = 'high'
    current_value = row['swing_high']
  elif not np.isnan(row['swing_low']):
    current_type = 'low'
    current_value = row['swing_low']
  else:
    continue
  if last_swing_type and current_type != last_swing_type:
    if current_type == 'low':
      # last was high → current is low
      my_time_series.at[i, 'resistance'] = ((last_swing_value - current_value) * fib_level) + current_value
    else:
      # last was low → current is high
      my_time_series.at[i, 'support'] = current_value - ((current_value - last_swing_value) * fib_level)
  last_swing_type = current_type
  last_swing_value = current_value
return my_time_series
```

Figure 5.6 shows a few signals generated by the code.

Figure 5.6 The reintegration technique. Support levels in gray and resistance levels in black

Swing highs and lows start to show their importance with this first simple algorithm. In subsequent chapters, you will see how to leverage their utility to more advanced technical tools. Some degree of look-ahead bias may be present in the algorithm; however, this is acceptable, as an analyst visually identifying Fibonacci retracements on a chart would inherently possess the same bias.

The 61.8% Reactionary Technique

According to classic technical analysis, approaching the 61.8% retracement level can yield a contrarian reaction. Here's how:

- During a bullish market with a bottom at point A, if a top is seen at point B and the market reaches 61.8% of the AB leg, a stabilization/recovery can be expected.
- During a bearish market with a top at point A, if a bottom is seen at point B and the market reaches 61.8% of the AB leg, a correction/weakness can be expected.

Figure 5.7 shows the assumption in a visual way.

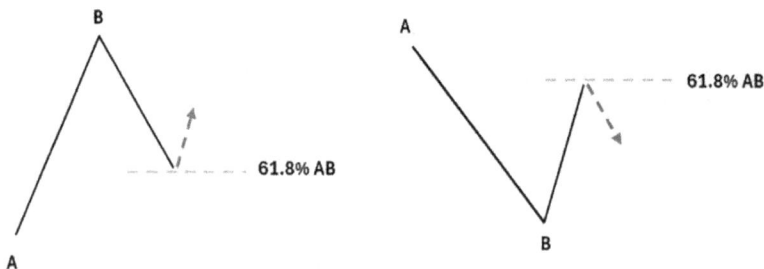

Figure 5.7 **A theoretical illustration of the reactionary technique**

In algorithmic language, here's how this technique works:

- Consider point A as a swing low and point B as a swing high. Calculating the difference between point A and point B, multiplying it by 0.618, and subtracting the total from point B will give the 61.8% support of AB. This is known as the 61.8% Fibonacci retracement of the AB point. It can also be referred to as the most important Fibonacci support level.
- Consider point A as a swing high and point B as a swing low. Calculating the difference between point A and point B, multiplying it by 0.618, and adding the total to point B will give the 61.8% resistance of AB. This is known as the 61.8% Fibonacci retracement of the AB point. It can also be referred to as the most important Fibonacci resistance level.

The only change you'll make to the above code is the fib_level variable, which will now be set to 0.618. Figure 5.8 shows a few signals generated by the code.

Figure 5.8 The reactionary technique. Support levels in gray *and resistance levels in* black

Remember, you can access the code in the GitHub repository. For now, focus on understanding the concepts. In Chapter 12, you will get to understand performance evaluation in detail, which you can use to backtest these techniques. This chapter presented two classic assumptions from plain vanilla technical analysis. We have added a modern touch by creating two algorithms to detect them through a rules-based method with the help of swing points.

CHAPTER 6

Advanced Volatility Indicators

Volatility is a fundamental concept in time series analysis. It represents the degree of variation or dispersion in a set of values over time, capturing the uncertainty or risk inherent in the data. Understanding and measuring volatility is crucial for a myriad of applications, including risk management and forecasting. There are many ways to measure (or approximate) volatility, and this chapter discusses several of them. But first, what is the utility of volatility to you as a trader? The first thing that comes to mind should be risk management through these three main facets:

- Volatility helps in determining the size of trading positions. Higher volatility suggests larger potential price swings, leading traders to reduce position sizes to manage risk.
- Setting stop-loss[7] levels based on volatility helps to ensure that stops are not too tight (resulting in premature exits) or too loose (leading to larger losses).
- Understanding the volatility of different assets enables you to diversify your portfolios effectively, reducing overall risk by balancing volatile and stable assets.

Additionally, volatility is also useful in trading strategies, meaning that it can have an added value with respect to predictive analytics:

- Volatility analysis can help you decide when to enter or exit the market. Periods of low volatility might indicate a potential breakout, while high volatility could suggest caution.

---

[7]A stop loss is a predetermined price level at which a trader exits a position to limit potential losses. It helps manage risk by automatically closing a trade when the market moves unfavorably.

- Volatility patterns can assist you in identifying trends and potential reversals. A sudden increase in volatility might signal a trend
  change or the beginning of a new trend.

Let's discover how to measure volatility using several techniques.

Standard Deviation

Descriptive statistics brought us the concept of variance and standard deviation, two related concepts for data variability around a mean. Consider
the following list:

$$\{1,1,1,1,1\}$$

What would you say about the fluctuations of the values around the
mean of the list? If your answer was zero, then you're right. Intuitively, the
list only contains the value 1. Therefore, the mean of the list must be 1. If
all the values are equal to 1 and the mean is 1, then the volatility (fluctu-
ation around the mean) is naturally 0. For the sake of doing things right,
let's see how to calculate standard deviation mathematically:

1. Calculate the mean of the data using the following formula:

$$\mu = \frac{1}{n}\sum_{i=1}^{n}x_i$$

2. Subtract the mean from each data point to find the deviation of
   each data point.
3. Square each deviation to eliminate negative values and emphasize
   larger deviations.
4. Add all the squared deviations together and calculate the average to
   find the variance.

$$\sigma^2 = \frac{1}{N}\sum_{i=1}^{N}(x_i - \mu)^2$$

5. The standard deviation is the square root of the variance.

$$\sigma = \sqrt{\sigma^2} = \sqrt{\frac{1}{N}\sum_{i=1}^{N}(x_i - \mu)^2}$$

By taking the elements from the previous list, we will have the following calculations:

$$\mu = \frac{1+1+1+1+1}{5} = 1$$

$$\sigma^2 = \frac{1}{5}\sum(1-1)^2 = 0$$

$$\sigma = \sqrt{\sigma^2} = 0$$

When dealing with time series such as stock prices, we may be interested in calculating the rolling volatility. This means that we will have another time series that is parallel to the first one but calculates the standard deviation of the most recent values given a rolling window (e.g., the standard deviation of the last 14 values). With every new value added to the list, such as a new tick getting recorded, the standard deviation calculation updates it by adding the recent value and by dropping the first value so that the rolling window remains unchanged. The following block shows how to define and calculate a rolling standard deviation measure:

```
def standard_deviation(my_time_series, source='close', vol_lookback=20):
    my_time_series['volatility'] = my_time_series[source].rolling(window=vol_lookback).std()
    return my_time_series.dropna()
```

Figure 6.1 shows an example of a rolling standard deviation.

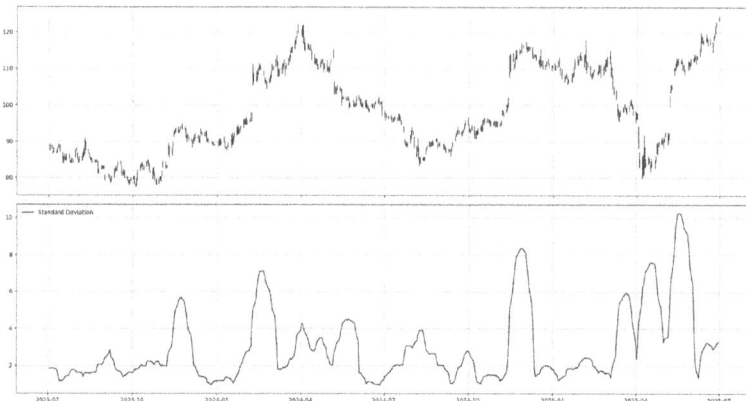

Figure 6.1 Standard deviation

Volatility, as measured by standard deviation, tends to have a slightly negative correlation with the underlying asset's price. When a stock price is steadily increasing, it often reflects investor confidence and reduced uncertainty. In such periods of stability, the price movements are smoother and less erratic. Reduced price fluctuations lead to a lower rolling standard deviation (volatility). Conversely, when a stock price is declining, it can indicate increased uncertainty or negative sentiment among investors. During such periods, prices may experience more significant swings due to panic selling, speculation, and other market reactions. These larger price swings increase the rolling standard deviation, reflecting higher volatility.

Exponentially Weighted Standard Deviation

The standard deviation calculated using an EMA will be more sensitive to recent changes in the data. This can be useful where more recent data is considered more relevant. In other words, the calculation of volatility will be more up-to-date when compared to the one calculated using the SMA. Exponentially weighted standard deviation (EWSD) can be computed as follows:

- Calculate the EMA of the price.
- Calculate the variance using the EMA:

$$\sigma_t^2 = \alpha(x_t - \text{EMA}_{t-1})^2 + (1 - \alpha)\sigma_{t-1}^2$$

- Calculate the standard deviation as the square root of the previous step (variance):

$$\sigma_t = \sqrt{\sigma^2}$$

By following these steps, you can compute EWSD, which will provide a more responsive measure of volatility compared to the SMA-based standard deviation. The following block shows how to define and calculate EWSD:

```
def exponentially_weighted_standard_deviation(my_time_series,
source='close', vol_lookback=20):
    my_time_series['volatility'] = my_time_series[source].ewm(span=vol_
lookback, adjust=False).std()
    return my_time_series.dropna()
```

Figure 6.2 shows the plot of EWSD.

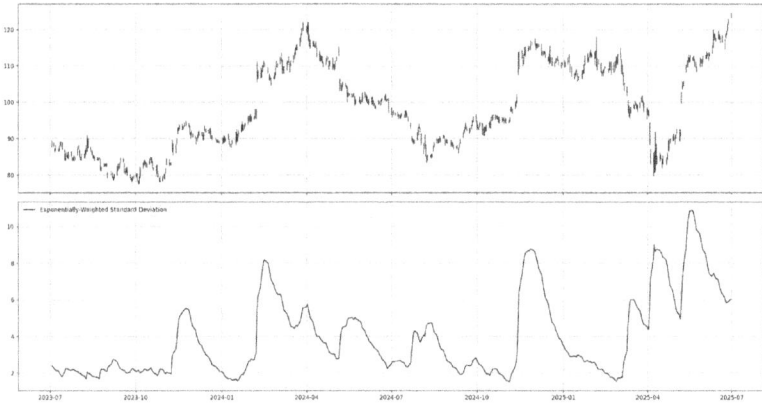

Figure 6.2 Exponentially weighted standard deviation

We have seen how to calculate a rolling standard deviation method in order to represent a time series' volatility through two ways, the original way and the exponentially weighted way. The original way is sensitive to all past data equally, which can make it less responsive to recent changes. In contrast, EWSD is more responsive to recent changes.

The Average True Range

The average true range (ATR) measures market volatility in a more straightforward way than its predecessors in this chapter. It was introduced by J. Welles Wilder in 1978, the inventor of the RSI. Unlike other volatility indicators that focus solely on price changes, the ATR considers the degree of price movement, including gaps. It's especially useful to set stop-loss and profit levels.

The ATR is based on the true range (TR) for a given window, typically 14 periods. The TR is the maximum of the following three values at any given time step:

- The difference between the current high and the current low
- The difference between the current high and the previous close
- The difference between the current low and the previous close

Mathematically, we can represent the TR as follows:

$$TR_i = \max(\text{High}_i - \text{low}_i, |\ \text{high}_i - \text{close}_{t-1}\ |, |\ \text{low}_i, \text{close}_{t-1}\ |)$$

The ATR is the SMMA of the TR. A high ATR value indicates high volatility and large price movements, whereas a low ATR value indicates low volatility and small price movements. It's important to remember that the ATR does not indicate price direction, only the degree of price volatility, and thus, must be treated as you would treat the previous volatility indicators. The following block shows how to define and calculate the ATR.

```
def atr(my_time_series, vol_lookback=20):
    # create a column containing the previous close prices
    my_time_series['previous_close'] = my_time_series['close'].shift(1)
    # calculate the true range
    my_time_series['TR'] = my_time_series.apply(lambda row: max(row['high'] - row['low'],
                            abs(row['high'] - row['previous_close']),
                            abs(row['low'] - row['previous_close'])), axis=1)
    # transform the lookback to fit a smoothed moving average
    vol_lookback = (vol_lookback * 2) - 1
    # calculate the atr
    my_time_series['volatility'] = my_time_series['TR'].ewm(span=vol_lookback, adjust=False).mean()
    my_time_series = my_time_series.drop(columns=['previous_close', 'TR'])
    return my_time_series.dropna()
```

Figure 6.3 shows ATR in action.

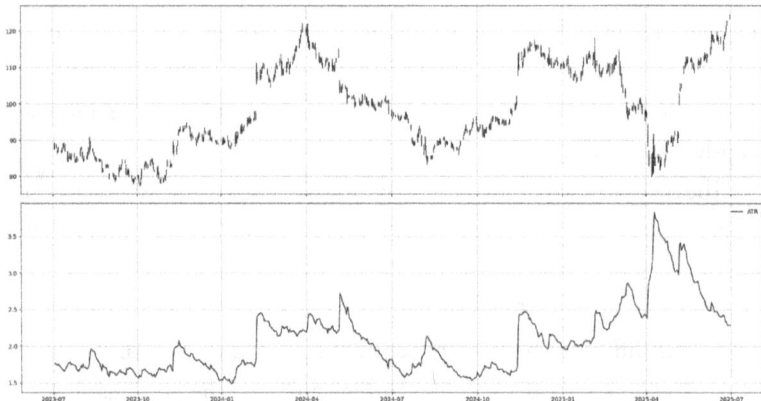

Figure 6.3 **ATR**

The Spike-Weighted Volatility

The spike-weighted volatility (SWV) enhances traditional rolling volatility (like rolling standard deviation) by giving extra weight to price spikes, making it responsive during turbulent market conditions without overreacting during normal swings. The core idea is to combine rolling standard deviation with a spike sensitivity factor, which measures how extreme a return is compared to recent history—dynamically weighting it into the volatility. Let:

- r_t: the return at time t
- μ_t: the mean of returns over the lookback
- σ_t: the standard deviation of returns over the lookback
- s_t: the spike factor as a function of the z-score of returns
- w: the lookback (window)

SWV at time t is given by the following formula:

$$\text{SWV}_t = \sqrt{\frac{1}{w} \sum_{i=t-w+1}^{t} (r_i^2 \cdot (1 + s_i))}$$

The returns are therefore squared and weighted by the magnitude of their spike (z-score). This makes high-volatility periods contribute more to the total without being binary. It's worth noting that the z-score measures how far a value is from the mean, in terms of standard deviations. In other words, it tells you how unusual or extreme a value is compared to recent data:

- A z-score of 0 means it's right at the average.
- A z-score of +2 means it's two standard deviations above the average (unusually high).
- A z-score of −2 means it's two standard deviations below the average (unusually low).

Use the following function to implement the SWV.

```
def spike_weighted_volatility(my_time_series, source='close',
vol_lookback=20):
  returns = my_time_series[source].pct_change()
  mean_returns = returns.rolling(vol_lookback).mean()
```

```
std_returns = returns.rolling(vol_lookback).std()
spike_factor = np.abs(returns - mean_returns) / (std_returns + 1e-8)
weighted_squared = (returns ** 2) * (1 + spike_factor)
aswv = np.sqrt(weighted_squared.rolling(vol_lookback).mean())
my_time_series['swv'] = aswv
return my_time_series.dropna()
```

Typically, SWV reacts smoothly to volatility spikes but filters noise. It's also excellent for volatility-aware position sizing or dynamic stop-loss adjustments. Figure 6.4 shows an example of the SWV.

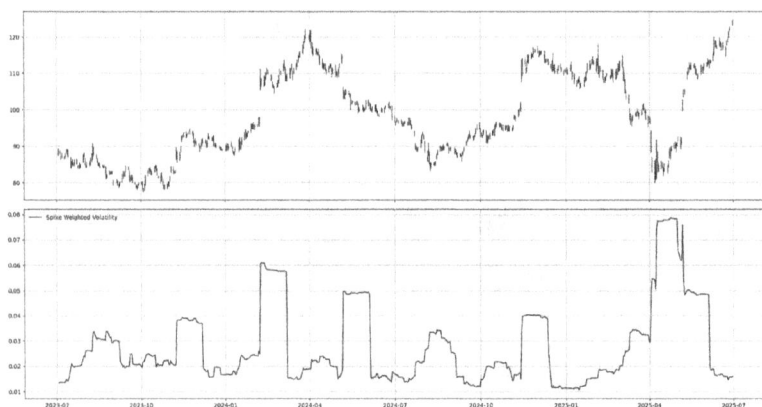

Figure 6.4 Spike-weighted volatility

Each SWV value represents the spike-adjusted standard deviation of recent percentage returns over the given window. If $SWV = 0.015$, it means that over the last lookback (e.g., 20 days), the average spike-weighted return volatility was about 1.5% daily. The SWV tells you not just how volatile the market is, but whether that volatility includes spike pressure—often associated with emotional or news-driven behavior. The SWV value provides insight into market behavior based on recent price action. Even though it varies through asset classes, when SWV is between approximately 0.002 and 0.005, the market is very quiet, indicating tight price action and a higher likelihood of mean-reverting behavior. Values in the range of 0.005 to 0.015 suggest normal volatility, typically associated with routine market noise and the potential for trend continuation. When SWV rises to around 0.015 to 0.03, it signals increased volatility, often seen during breakouts, strong directional moves, or corrective phases. Values above 0.03 reflect highly volatile and unstable conditions, usually driven by news events, panic selling, or extreme speculative activity.

The Volatility Index

The volatility index (VIX) is a widely recognized measure of the stock market's expectation of volatility over the next 30 days. Commonly referred to as the fear index, VIX provides insight into market sentiment, particularly the level of fear or complacency among investors. It was introduced in 1993 by the Chicago Board Options Exchange (CBOE). VIX is calculated using the prices of S&P 500 index options, including both calls and puts, to capture market expectations of future volatility. The formula of VIX is complex, but it essentially averages the weighted prices of multiple options to estimate the expected 30-day volatility of the S&P 500. Here's how to interpret this index:

- A high VIX indicates increased market volatility and uncertainty. Historically, a high VIX value is associated with market downturns or crises, as investors expect larger price swings.
- A low VIX suggests lower market volatility and greater stability. A low VIX value typically corresponds with bullish market sentiment and less perceived risk.

Traders often speculate on future market volatility by taking positions in VIX-related financial instruments. For example, traders expecting a bearish market and increased volatility may buy VIX futures or exchange-traded funds (ETFs). VIX has experienced significant spikes during major market events, such as the 2008 financial crisis, the Eurozone debt crisis, and the COVID-19 pandemic. Each spike represents a period of heightened fear and uncertainty among investors, often coinciding with sharp market declines. How does VIX relate to technical analysis? VIX is simply another time series that benefits from the application of technical indicators and methods on it. For example, applying the RSI on VIX can give you another image of equities. Imagine having a bullish signal from the RSI on the S&P 500 index, and at the same time, there is a bearish signal from the RSI on VIX. This will add further conviction to your bullish equities idea. Figure 6.5 shows the application of a 5-period RSI on VIX.

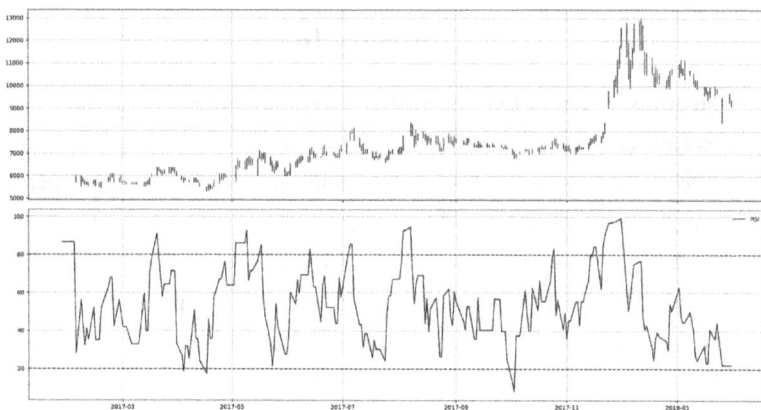

Figure 6.5 RSI applied to VIX values

In summary, each method has its strengths and ideal application scenarios, highlighting the importance of choosing the appropriate estimator based on the specific characteristics of the data and the underlying asset.

## CHAPTER 7

Pattern Recognition in Python I—Candlestick Patterns

A pattern can be defined as a recurring sequence of events that can be observed and analyzed to predict future occurrences or behaviors. Patterns can be found in various contexts, such as art, mathematics, and markets. In general, a pattern provides a sense of regularity and predictability, allowing us to recognize relationships and trends within a given dataset or environment. In the context of financial markets, patterns refer to specific formations or sequences in the market. These patterns attempt to forecast future price movements. This chapter inaugurates the pattern recognition part of the book by introducing candlesticks from a different angle. Classic candlestick patterns can be found online. In this chapter, you will learn about modern candlestick patterns and how to properly code and visualize them. But before that, you will see an example of a classic candlestick pattern (the Doji pattern) in order to familiarize yourself with this type of configuration.

Detecting the Doji Pattern

The Doji pattern occurs whenever the open and close prices are very close or equal, indicating indecision in the market and a possible halt in the current move. A bullish market will generally have big bullish candlesticks pushing prices higher. At one point in time, the bullish momentum will start to fade, and the candlesticks will start to get smaller and begin resembling Doji patterns. This is where traders start to anticipate a market correction or a reversal. In contrast, a bearish market will generally have big bearish candlesticks pushing prices lower. Arriving at the bottom of the market, we may start seeing a few Doji candlesticks, which may hint toward a possible recovery. The conditions of the Doji pattern are as follows:

- The bullish Doji pattern is composed of a bearish candlestick followed by a Doji candlestick and a bullish candlestick for confirmation. It should occur during a downtrend.
- The bearish Doji pattern is composed of a bullish candlestick followed by a Doji candlestick and a bearish candlestick for confirmation. It should occur during an uptrend.

Take a look at Figure 7.1, which illustrates the theoretical Doji pattern.

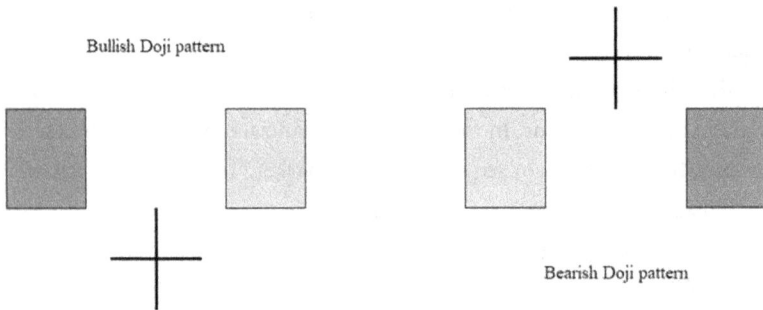

Figure 7.1 Doji pattern

The following code block shows how to create the algorithm that detects the pattern.

```python
def doji(my_time_series):
  my_time_series['bullish_signal'] = 0
  my_time_series['bearish_signal'] = 0
  for i in range(0, len(my_time_series)):
    try:
      # bullish signal
      if my_time_series['close'].iloc[i-2] < my_time_series['open'].iloc[i-2] and \
        my_time_series['close'].iloc[i-1] == my_time_series['open'].iloc[i-1] and \
        my_time_series['close'].iloc[i] > my_time_series['open'].iloc[i]:
          my_time_series.at[my_time_series.index[i+1], 'bullish_signal'] = 1
      # bearish signal
      elif my_time_series['close'].iloc[i-2] > my_time_series['open'].iloc[i-2] and \
        my_time_series['close'].iloc[i-1] == my_time_series['open'].iloc[i-1] and \
        my_time_series['close'].iloc[i] < my_time_series['open'].iloc[i]:
```

```
        my_time_series.at[my_time_series.index[i+1], 'bearish_signal'] = 1
    except KeyError:
        pass
return my_time_series
```

The following chart shows a few signals generated by the algorithm (Figure 7.2).

Figure 7.2 Signal chart highlighting Doji patterns

It's also possible to see bullish Doji patterns in a bullish trend and bearish Doji patterns in a bearish trend. On its own, a Doji doesn't guarantee a reversal—it just tells you the market is hesitating. Think of it as a yellow light, not a red or green one.

Detecting the R Pattern

The R pattern is a structured modern configuration that requires the help of an exogenous indicator, the RSI. The R pattern got its name from the first letter of the RSI, and is a modern reversal pattern that incorporates the highs and lows as well as the close price in its conditions:

- The bullish R pattern is composed of four candlesticks where the latest low is greater than the previous low, the previous low is greater than the prior low, and the prior low is less than the one before it. The closing price must be increasing. Additionally, the 14-period RSI must be below 50%.

- The bearish R pattern is composed of four candlesticks where the latest high is less than the previous high, the previous high is less than the prior high, and the prior high is greater than the one before it. The closing price must be decreasing. Additionally, the 14-period RSI must be above 50%.

Take a look at Figure 7.3, which illustrates the theoretical R pattern.

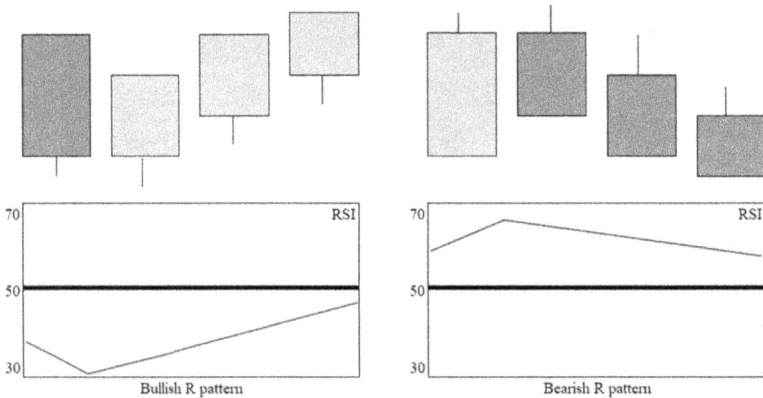

Bullish R pattern   Bearish R pattern

Figure 7.3 R pattern

The following code block shows how to create the algorithm that detects the pattern.

```
def r(my_time_series):
  my_time_series = rsi(my_time_series, source='close', rsi_lookback=14)
  my_time_series['bullish_signal'] = 0
  my_time_series['bearish_signal'] = 0
  for i in range(0, len(my_time_series)):
    try:
     # bullish signal
     if my_time_series['low'].iloc[i] > my_time_series['low'].iloc[i-1] and \
       my_time_series['low'].iloc[i-1] > my_time_series['low'].iloc[i-2] and \
       my_time_series['low'].iloc[i-2] < my_time_series['low'].iloc[i-3] and \
       my_time_series['close'].iloc[i] > my_time_series['close'].iloc[i-1] and \
       my_time_series['close'].iloc[i-1] > my_time_series['close'].iloc[i-2] and \
       my_time_series['close'].iloc[i-2] > my_time_series['close'].iloc[i-3] and \
       my_time_series['RSI'].iloc[i] < 50:
        my_time_series.at[my_time_series.index[i+1], 'bullish_signal'] = 1
     # bearish signal
     elif my_time_series['high'].iloc[i] < my_time_series['high'].iloc[i-1] and \
       my_time_series['high'].iloc[i-1] < my_time_series['high'].iloc[i-2] and \
```

```
      my_time_series['high'].iloc[i-2] > my_time_series['high'].iloc[i-3] and \
      my_time_series['close'].iloc[i] < my_time_series['close'].iloc[i-1] and \
      my_time_series['close'].iloc[i-1] < my_time_series['close'].iloc[i-2] and \
      my_time_series['close'].iloc[i-2] < my_time_series['close'].iloc[i-3] and \
      my_time_series['RSI'].iloc[i] > 50:
        my_time_series.at[my_time_series.index[i+1], 'bearish_signal'] = 1
   except KeyError:
     pass
 return my_time_series
```

Figure 7.4 shows a few signals generated by the algorithm.

Figure 7.4 Signal chart highlighting R patterns

The R configuration is not a timing pattern, as it signals intermediate reversals that also draw on the RSI's strength to detect the current momentum, which may occur with a certain delay.

Detecting the Bottle Pattern

The Bottle pattern is a modern continuation configuration that hints toward increased current momentum. The conditions of the patterns are as follows:

- The bullish Bottle pattern is composed of a bullish candle followed by another bullish candle with no wick on the low side but with a wick on the high side. At the same time, the second candle must open below the last candle's close (gap lower).

- The bearish Bottle pattern is composed of a bearish candlestick followed by another bearish candle with no wick on the high side but with a wick on the low side. At the same time, the second candle must open above the last candle's close (gap higher).

Take a look at the following theoretical illustration highlighting the pattern (Figure 7.5).

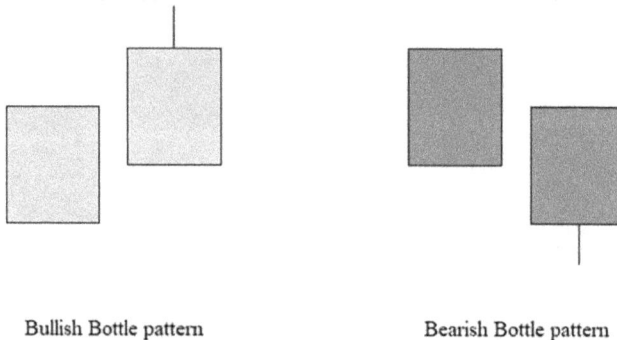

Bullish Bottle pattern   Bearish Bottle pattern

Figure 7.5 Bottle pattern

The following code block shows how to create the algorithm that detects the pattern.

```
def bottle(my_time_series):
  my_time_series['bullish_signal'] = 0
  my_time_series['bearish_signal'] = 0
  for i in range(0, len(my_time_series)):
    try:
     # bullish signal
     if my_time_series['close'].iloc[i] > my_time_series['open'].iloc[i] and \
       my_time_series['open'].iloc[i] == my_time_series['low'].iloc[i] and \
       my_time_series['close'].iloc[i-1] > my_time_series['open'].iloc[i-1] and \
       my_time_series['open'].iloc[i-1] < my_time_series['close'].iloc[i-1]:
         my_time_series.at[my_time_series.index[i+1], 'bullish_signal'] = 1
     # bearish signal
     elif my_time_series['close'].iloc[i] < my_time_series['open'].iloc[i] and \
       my_time_series['open'].iloc[i] == my_time_series['high'].iloc[i] and \
       my_time_series['close'].iloc[i-1] < my_time_series['open'].iloc[i-1] and \
       my_time_series['open'].iloc[i-1] > my_time_series['close'].iloc[i-1]:
         my_time_series.at[my_time_series.index[i+1], 'bearish_signal'] = 1
```

```
except KeyError:
  pass
return my_time_series
```

Figure 7.6 shows a few signals generated by the algorithm.

Figure 7.6 Signal chart highlighting Bottle patterns

Detecting the Double Trouble Pattern

The double trouble pattern is a modern continuation configuration that relies on the ATR to validate its conditions. Remember, the ATR is a volatility measure that uses high, low, and close prices to deliver a proxy of the market volatility. The conditions of the pattern are as follows:

- The bullish double trouble pattern is composed of two bullish candles with the second candle having a close price greater than the close price of the first candle. Additionally, the size of the second candle must be larger than twice the value of the last ATR value.
- The bearish double trouble pattern is composed of two bearish candles with the second candle having a close price below the close price of the first candle. Additionally, the size of the second candle must be larger than twice the value of the last ATR value.

Take a look at the following theoretical illustration highlighting the pattern (Figure 7.7).

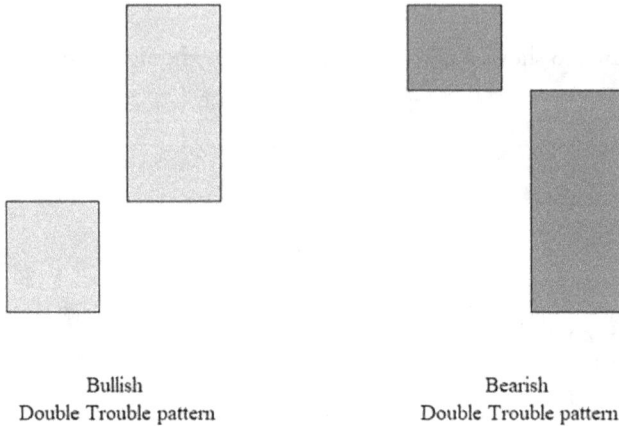

Bullish
Double Trouble pattern

Bearish
Double Trouble pattern

Figure 7.7 Double trouble pattern

The following code block shows how to create the algorithm that detects the pattern.

```
def double_trouble(my_time_series):
  my_time_series['bullish_signal'] = 0
  my_time_series['bearish_signal'] = 0
  my_time_series = atr(my_time_series, vol_lookback=14)
  for i in range(0, len(my_time_series)):
    try:
      # bullish signal
      if my_time_series['close'].iloc[i] > my_time_series['open'].iloc[i] and \
        my_time_series['close'].iloc[i-1] > my_time_series['open'].iloc[i-1] and \
        my_time_series['close'].iloc[i] > my_time_series['close'].iloc[i-1] and \
        (my_time_series['close'].iloc[i] - my_time_series['open'].iloc[i]) > (2 *
                        my_time_series['volatility'].iloc[i-1]):
        my_time_series.at[my_time_series.index[i+1], 'bullish_signal'] = 1
      # bearish signal
      elif my_time_series['close'].iloc[i] < my_time_series['open'].iloc[i] and \
        my_time_series['close'].iloc[i-1] < my_time_series['open'].iloc[i-1] and \
        my_time_series['close'].iloc[i] < my_time_series['close'].iloc[i-1] and \
        (my_time_series['open'].iloc[i] - my_time_series['close'].iloc[i]) > (2 *
                        my_time_series['volatility'].iloc[i-1]):
        my_time_series.at[my_time_series.index[i+1], 'bearish_signal'] = 1
    except KeyError:
      pass
  return my_time_series
```

Figure 7.8 shows a few signals generated by the algorithm.

Figure 7.8 Signal chart highlighting double trouble patterns

To conclude, the double trouble pattern is a trend-following config-uration that uses an exogenous volatility indicator to confirm the signals. As with every trend-following technique, it can have an inherent lag fac-tor, and thus, it must be handled with care.

Detecting the Extreme Euphoria Pattern

The extreme euphoria pattern is a modern reversal configuration com-posed of five candlesticks. The conditions of the patterns are as follows:

- The bullish extreme euphoria pattern is composed of five bearish candlesticks with increasing sizes (especially the last two candles).
- The bearish extreme euphoria pattern is composed of five bullish candlesticks with increasing sizes (especially the last two candles).

Take a look at the following theoretical illustration highlighting the pattern (Figure 7.9).

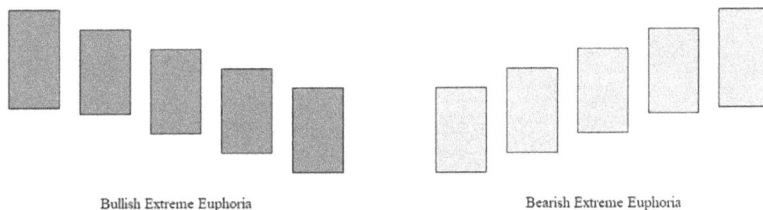

Bullish Extreme Euphoria   Bearish Extreme Euphoria

Figure 7.9 Extreme euphoria pattern

The following code block shows how to create the algorithm that detects the pattern.

```python
def extreme_euphoria(my_time_series):
  my_time_series['bullish_signal'] = 0
  my_time_series['bearish_signal'] = 0
  my_time_series['absolute_range'] = abs(my_time_series['close'] - my_time_series['open'])
  for i in range(0, len(my_time_series)):
    try:
      # bullish signal
      if my_time_series['close'].iloc[i] < my_time_series['open'].iloc[i] and \
        my_time_series['close'].iloc[i-1] < my_time_series['open'].iloc[i-1] and \
        my_time_series['close'].iloc[i-2] < my_time_series['open'].iloc[i-2] and \
        my_time_series['close'].iloc[i-3] < my_time_series['open'].iloc[i-3] and \
        my_time_series['close'].iloc[i-4] < my_time_series['open'].iloc[i-4] and \
        my_time_series['absolute_range'].iloc[i] > my_time_series['absolute_range'].iloc[i-1] and \
        my_time_series['absolute_range'].iloc[i-1] > my_time_series['absolute_range'].iloc[i-2]:
          my_time_series.at[my_time_series.index[i+1], 'bullish_signal'] = 1
      # bearish signal
      elif my_time_series['close'].iloc[i] > my_time_series['open'].iloc[i] and \
        my_time_series['close'].iloc[i-1] > my_time_series['open'].iloc[i-1] and \
        my_time_series['close'].iloc[i-2] > my_time_series['open'].iloc[i-2] and \
        my_time_series['close'].iloc[i-3] > my_time_series['open'].iloc[i-3] and \
        my_time_series['close'].iloc[i-4] > my_time_series['open'].iloc[i-4] and \
        my_time_series['absolute_range'].iloc[i] > my_time_series['absolute_range'].iloc[i-1] and \
        my_time_series['absolute_range'].iloc[i-1] > my_time_series['absolute_range'].iloc[i-2]:
          my_time_series.at[my_time_series.index[i+1], 'bearish_signal'] = 1
    except KeyError:
      pass
  return my_time_series
```

Figure 7.10 shows a few signals generated by the algorithm.

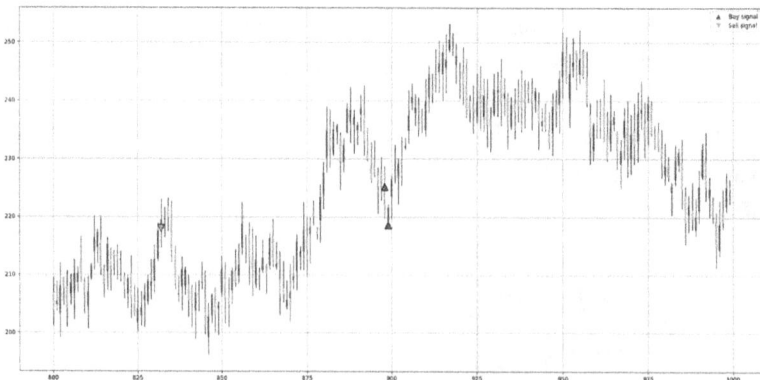

Figure 7.10 Signal chart highlighting extreme euphoria patterns

CARSI Patterns

In Chapter 4, you have learned about CARSI, an application of OHLC candlestick analysis on the RSI. This section will apply another selection of modern candlestick patterns on CARSI.

Hidden Shovel Pattern

The next pattern is the hidden shovel that has the following conditions:

- A bullish signal is generated whenever the current Low_{RSI} value is below 30 and the three remaining RSI values are above 30. Additionally, the previous Low_{RSI} value is above 30.
- A bearish signal is generated whenever the current $High_{RSI}$ value is above 70 and the three remaining RSI values are below 70. Additionally, the previous $High_{RSI}$ value is below 70.

Take a look at the following theoretical illustration highlighting the pattern (Figure 7.11).

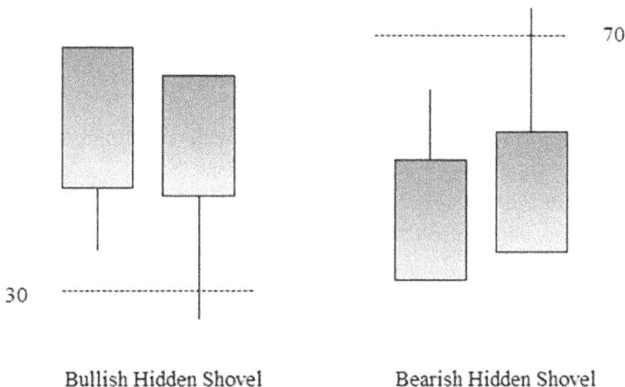

Bullish Hidden Shovel   Bearish Hidden Shovel

Figure 7.11 Hidden shovel pattern

Figure 7.12 shows a few signals generated by the algorithm.

Figure 7.12 Signal chart highlighting hidden shovel patterns

The following code block shows how to create the algorithm that detects the pattern.

```python
def hidden_shovel(my_time_series):
  my_time_series = candlestick_rsi(my_time_series, rsi_lookback=14)
  my_time_series['bullish_signal'] = 0
  my_time_series['bearish_signal'] = 0
  for i in range(0, len(my_time_series)):
    try:
      # bullish signal
      if my_time_series['RSI_low'].iloc[i] < 30 and \
        my_time_series['RSI_close'].iloc[i] > 30 and \
        my_time_series['RSI_open'].iloc[i] > 30 and \
        my_time_series['RSI_high'].iloc[i] > 30 and \
        my_time_series['RSI_low'].iloc[i-1] > 30:
          my_time_series.at[my_time_series.index[i+1], 'bullish_signal'] = 1
      # bearish signal
      elif my_time_series['RSI_high'].iloc[i] > 70 and \
        my_time_series['RSI_close'].iloc[i] < 70 and \
        my_time_series['RSI_open'].iloc[i] < 70 and \
        my_time_series['RSI_low'].iloc[i] < 70 and \
        my_time_series['RSI_high'].iloc[i-1] < 70:
          my_time_series.at[my_time_series.index[i+1], 'bearish_signal'] = 1
    except KeyError:
      pass
  return my_time_series
```

Absolute U-Turn Pattern

The next pattern is the absolute U-turn that has the following conditions:

- A bullish signal is generated whenever the current Low_{RSI} value is above 20 while the last five Low_{RSI} values are below 20.
- A bearish signal is generated whenever the current $High_{RSI}$ value is below 80 while the last five $High_{RSI}$ values are above 80.

Take a look at the following theoretical illustration highlighting the pattern (Figure 7.13).

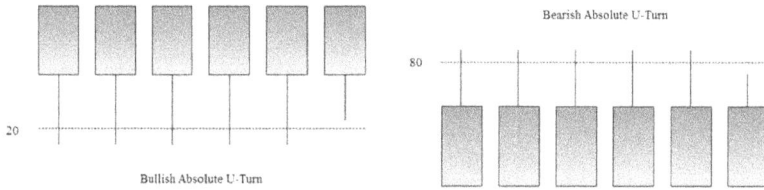

Figure 7.13 Absolute U-turn pattern

The following code block shows how to create the algorithm that detects the pattern.

```
def absolute_u_turn(my_time_series):
  my_time_series = candlestick_rsi(my_time_series, rsi_lookback=14)
  my_time_series['bullish_signal'] = 0
  my_time_series['bearish_signal'] = 0
  for i in range(0, len(my_time_series)):
    try:
      # bullish signal
      if my_time_series['RSI_low'].iloc[i] > 20 and \
        my_time_series['RSI_low'].iloc[i-1] < 20 and \
        my_time_series['RSI_low'].iloc[i-2] < 20 and \
        my_time_series['RSI_low'].iloc[i-3] < 20 and \
        my_time_series['RSI_low'].iloc[i-4] < 20 and \
        my_time_series['RSI_low'].iloc[i-5] < 20:
          my_time_series.at[my_time_series.index[i+1], 'bullish_signal'] = 1
      # bearish signal
      elif my_time_series['RSI_high'].iloc[i] < 80 and \
        my_time_series['RSI_high'].iloc[i-1] > 80 and \
```

```
    my_time_series['RSI_high'].iloc[i-2] > 80 and \
    my_time_series['RSI_high'].iloc[i-3] > 80 and \
    my_time_series['RSI_high'].iloc[i-4] > 80 and \
    my_time_series['RSI_high'].iloc[i-5] > 80:
        my_time_series.at[my_time_series.index[i+1], 'bearish_signal'] = 1
    except KeyError:
        pass
return my_time_series
```

Figure 7.14 shows a few signals generated by the algorithm.

Figure 7.14 Signal chart highlighting absolute U-turn patterns (real data)

In conclusion, CARSI patterns are a set of configurations I have found to add predictive value in the framework of modern technical analysis. As with any other technical tools, they must be thoroughly back-tested on the asset you are interested in trading. This chapter inaugurated the pattern recognition algorithms with candlestick patterns, which may be considered as one of the simplest and most detectable market patterns. The efficacy of candlestick patterns in trading has been a topic of debate, with empirical research yielding mixed results. While classic patterns such as the Doji are widely recognized, studies suggest that their predictive power varies depending on market conditions, time frames, and asset classes. Some research indicates that candlestick patterns can offer a slight statistical edge when combined with other indicators or used in specific contexts, such as high-volatility environments or after strong trends, thus the birth of modern patterns that rely on exogenous indicators (the RSI and the ATR). However, standalone candlestick patterns often struggle to consistently outperform random chance (Figure 7.15).

Figure 7.15 Signal chart highlighting absolute U-turn patterns (simulated data)

CHAPTER 8

Pattern Recognition in Python II—Harmonic Patterns

Unlike traditional technical indicators that rely solely on moving averages, volume, or momentum, harmonic patterns are based on the recognition of specific price structures that adhere to mathematical ratios derived from Fibonacci sequences. The concept behind harmonic patterns is rooted in the idea that market movements are not random but rather follow specific cycles and patterns that can be identified and utilized for making trading decisions. These patterns suggest that prices move in waves and that these waves tend to repeat themselves over time, forming predictable structures. Harmonic patterns rely on the assumption that financial markets exhibit fractal behavior. This means that the patterns observed in small time frames can also be found in larger time frames, albeit in a more complex form. This fractal nature allows harmonic patterns to be applied across different markets and time frames. The term harmonic pattern refers to certain price configurations relying on Fibonacci retracements and projections in order to find potential reversal zones. They generally require a certain degree of subjectivity and discretion from the trader, but with the development of technology, it has become a duty to approach objectivity through rules-based algorithms. An alternative valid hypothesis as to why harmonic patterns are used is that they rely on the confluence of a number of Fibonacci retracements or projections. The next sections will present in detail a few harmonic patterns and how to code them in Python.

The ABCD Pattern

The ABCD pattern is the easiest and most frequent harmonic pattern, and it pertains to the concept of symmetry. The basic appearance is a zigzag line made out of four points in time (and thus, three lines), which form the pattern's name. For the ABCD pattern to be valid, the AB leg must equal the CD leg. Here's the rundown of this reversal pattern:

- The AB leg is impulsive and based on an initial move.
- The BC leg is corrective and based on a reactionary move.
- The CD leg is impulsive and based on a continuation of the initial move.
- The D point is the reversal zone from where the pattern becomes valid.

Figure 8.1 provides a theoretical illustration of the ABCD pattern. The price action does not have to be successive in order to achieve the ABCD pattern.

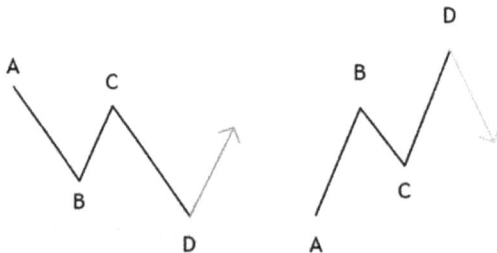

Figure 8.1 ABCD harmonic pattern

Ideally, you should start noticing the pattern halfway through the CD leg. This allows you to approximate the D point from where you would expect a corrective reaction and take action. The symmetry condition implies that this pattern does not rely on Fibonacci ratios per se. Note that symmetry refers to the equality between the AB and CD legs. The ABCD pattern is common and easily detectable. The clearer the pattern, the more likely it will provide a reaction, as more market participants will detect it and act on it. Use the following code to search for ABCD patterns.

```python
def abcd_pattern(my_time_series, swing_lookback=20):
    my_time_series = swing_detect(my_time_series, swing_lookback=swing_lookback)
    # initialize tracking variables
    prev1 = None
    prev2 = None
    prev3 = None
    # labeling
    for i, row in my_time_series.iterrows():
        if not pd.isna(row['swing_high']):
            swing_type = 'high'
            swing_value = row['swing_high']
        elif not pd.isna(row['swing_low']):
            swing_type = 'low'
            swing_value = row['swing_low']
        else:
            continue
        # skip if same type as previous swing
        if prev1 and swing_type == prev1[1]:
            continue
        # shift swings
        prev3 = prev2
        prev2 = prev1
        prev1 = (i, swing_type, swing_value)
        # check if we have 3 alternating swings to form ABC
        if prev3:
            A_i, A_type, A_val = prev3
            B_i, B_type, B_val = prev2
            C_i, C_type, C_val = prev1
            # bullish ABCD pattern: high → low → high → projecting low
            if A_type == 'high' and B_type == 'low' and C_type == 'high':
                if C_val <= A_val:
                    projection = C_val - (A_val - B_val)
                    my_time_series.at[C_i, 'bullish_signal'] = projection
            # bearish ABCD pattern: low → high → low → projecting high
            elif A_type == 'low' and B_type == 'high' and C_type == 'low':
                if C_val >= A_val:
                    projection = C_val + (B_val - A_val)
                    my_time_series.at[C_i, 'bearish_signal'] = projection
    return my_time_series
```

Figure 8.2 shows an oscillating time series where ABCD patterns are detected. The chart shows the following:

- The swing points detected by the **swing_detect** function. These help the algorithm find the key points from where to calculate the ABCD pattern.

- The support lines are in gray and the resistance lines are in black. These are found by supposing that the previous four alternating swing points are ABCD patterns, and thus, the lines are where the symmetry condition is met. Therefore, whenever the time series reaches the grey and black lines, a contrarian reaction is expected.

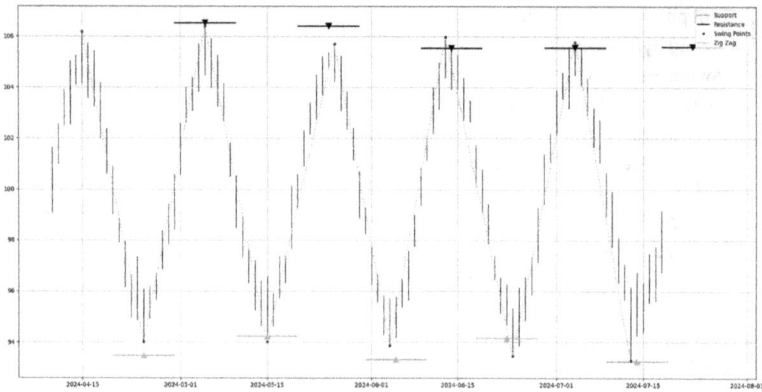

Figure 8.2 ABCD pattern detected on a generated almost symmetrical time series. Support levels in gray and resistance levels in black

Now, let's apply the `abcd_pattern` function on real data. Figure 8.3 shows detected ABCD patterns.

Figure 8.3 A first example of detected ABCD patterns. Support levels in gray and resistance levels in black

The different utilities of the algorithm can be summed up as follows:

- You can find the next ABCD support or resistance level by typing the following command: `print('Support at ', my_time_series['bullish_signal'][-1])` in case of a bullish ABCD or `print('Resistance at ', my_time_series['bearish_signal'][-1])` in case of a bearish ABCD. Or, you can simply look at the last value in the data frame (`bullish_signal` and `bearish_signal`).
- Visualize the past ABCD patterns to understand their efficacy and predictive value.
- Use the algorithm to back-test simple and complex strategies that use the ABCD pattern. You will learn how to create a performance evaluation function in Chapter 12.

The reactionary force from point D is considered to be more reliable when it's confirmed by the trend. This means the following:

- A bullish ABCD pattern in a bullish trend increases the conviction.
- A bearish ABCD pattern in a bearish trend increases the conviction.

To sum up, the ABCD pattern can be rendered less subjective through the use of an algorithm. Additionally, it can benefit from a trend enhancement filter that may enhance its predictive ability. Remember, you can adjust the sensitivity of the swing points you detect by tweaking the `swing_lookback` variable (more details on its impact can be found in Chapter 5). Figure 8.4 shows the same data frame as shown in Figure 8.4, but with a `lookback = 60`.

It's up to you to control the sensitivity of the ABCD pattern while keeping in mind that the key function is still `swing_detect`.

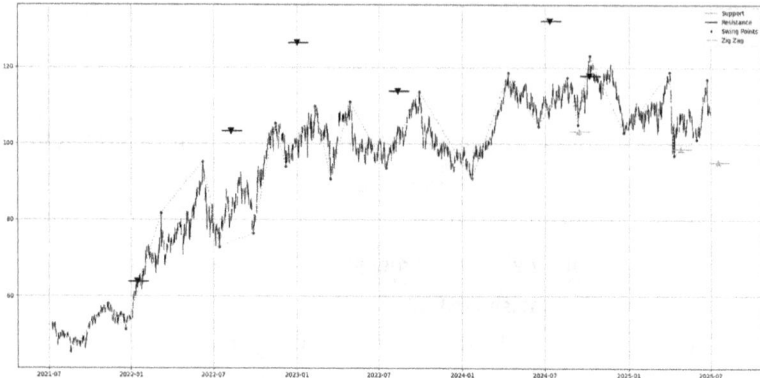

Figure 8.4 *A second example of detected ABCD patterns. Support levels in* gray *and resistance levels in* black

The Gartley Pattern

The Gartley pattern resembles a W-M setup and is a complex harmonic configuration. The basic appearance is the letter M for a bullish pattern and the letter W for a bearish pattern. The pattern is made out of five points in time (and thus, four lines). The points are called {X, A, B, C, D}. Here's the rundown of the pattern:

- The XA leg retraces back 61.8%, which forms point B.
- The AB leg retraces back 61.8%, which forms point C.
- The BC leg retraces back 161.8%, which forms point D (the reversal area).
- Point D must also be the 78.6% retracement of the XA leg.

Figure 8.5 provides a theoretical illustration of the Gartley pattern.

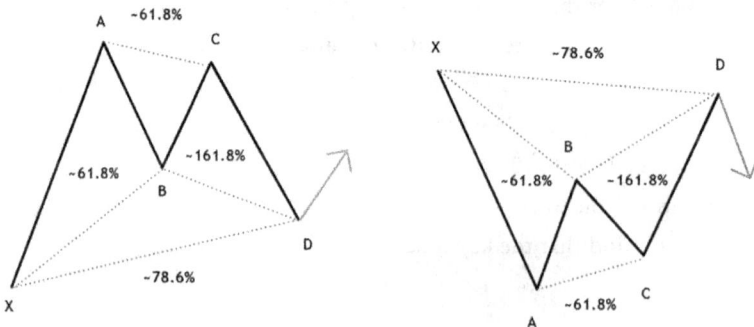

Figure 8.5 *Gartley pattern*

What makes the Gartley pattern is the confluence of the 161.8% and 78.6% ratios around the same area. Since, occasionally, the 78.6% serves as an excess[8] level over 61.8%, the Gartley pattern can be considered the perfect harmonic pattern composed of the golden ratio and its reciprocal, 61.8%. As you may have already noticed, there is an embedded ABCD pattern in the pattern. As the AB leg retraces back 61.8% and the BC leg retraces back 161.8%, the ABCD is considered perfect, which may add conviction to the reactionary zone around D. This is what makes the Gartley pattern very interesting as it's a combination of the perfect ABCD pattern with a retracement at 78.6% of the XA leg that may serve as a tolerance level over 61.8%. The concept of tolerance (excess) levels is important in analysis as markets generally do not form reactions at exactly one predefined point (e.g., the 61.8% retracement level), but around it. Use the following code to search for Gartley patterns.

```python
def detect_gartley_pattern(my_time_series, swing_lookback=20, fib_tolerance=3):
  my_time_series['bullish_signal'] = 0
  my_time_series['bearish_signal'] = 0
  my_time_series = swing_detect(my_time_series, swing_lookback=swing_lookback)
  swings = []
  for idx, row in my_time_series.iterrows():
    if not pd.isna(row['swing_high']):
      swings.append((idx, 'high', row['swing_high']))
    elif not pd.isna(row['swing_low']):
      swings.append((idx, 'low', row['swing_low']))
  for i in range(len(swings) - 4):
    p0, p1, p2, p3, p4 = swings[i:i+5]
    idx_x, type_x, px = p0
    idx_a, type_a, pa = p1
    idx_b, type_b, pb = p2
    idx_c, type_c, pc = p3
    idx_d, type_d, pd_ = p4
    if [type_x, type_a, type_b, type_c, type_d] == ['low', 'high', 'low', 'high', 'low']:
      xa = pa - px
      ab = pb - pa
      bc = pc - pb
      cd = pd_ - pc
      ad = pd_ - px
      if np.isclose(abs(ab) / abs(xa), 0.618, atol=fib_tolerance) and \
        0.382 <= abs(bc) / abs(ab) <= 0.886 and \
        1.27 <= abs(cd) / abs(bc) <= 1.618 and \
        np.isclose(abs(ad) / abs(xa), 0.786, atol=fib_tolerance) and \
```

---

[8]An excess level is defined as a margin of tolerance around a support or resistance level. For example, a support level at $100 can have an excess at $99.50 to allow for the short-term noise before seeing a reaction to the upside.

```
    pd_ >= px:
      my_time_series.loc[idx_d+1, 'bullish_signal'] = 1
    elif [type_x, type_a, type_b, type_c, type_d] == ['high', 'low', 'high', 'low', 'high']:
      xa = px - pa
      ab = pa - pb
      bc = pb - pc
      cd = pc - pd_
      ad = px - pd_
      if np.isclose(abs(ab) / abs(xa), 0.618, atol=fib_tolerance) and \
        0.382 <= abs(bc) / abs(ab) <= 0.886 and \
        1.27 <= abs(cd) / abs(bc) <= 1.618 and \
        np.isclose(abs(ad) / abs(xa), 0.786, atol=fib_tolerance) and \
        pd_ <= px:
        my_time_series.loc[idx_d+1, 'bearish_signal'] = 1
  return my_time_series
```

Figure 8.6 shows a bullish Gartley pattern.

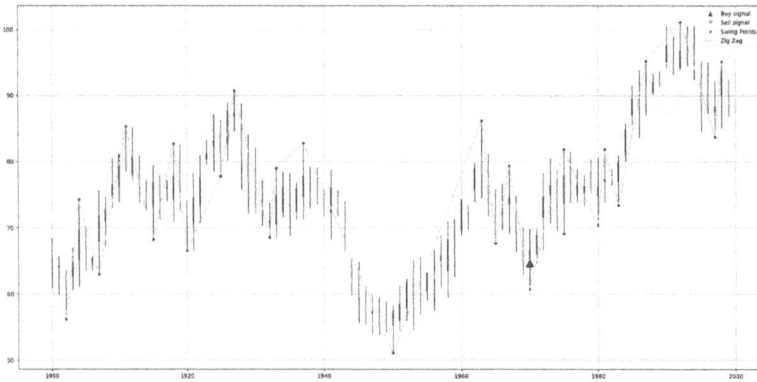

Figure 8.6 Signal chart showing a detected bullish Gartley

Figure 8.7 shows a bearish Gartley pattern.

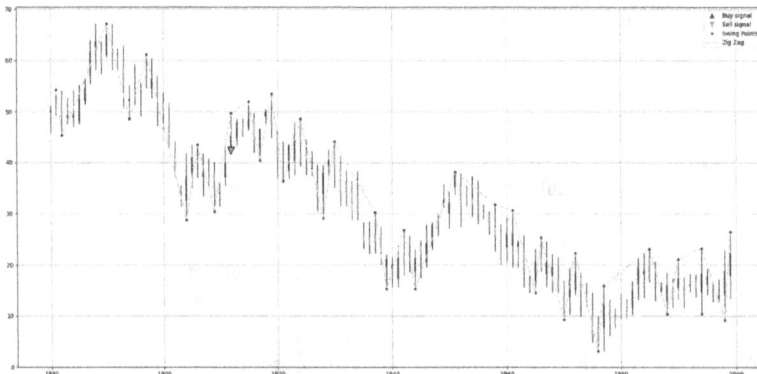

Figure 8.7 Signal chart showing a detected bearish Gartley

The Gartley pattern was first introduced by H.M. Gartley, a technical analyst, in his 1935 book, *Profits in the Stock Market*. The pattern was initially identified in Chapter 12 of his book, where he described it as a particularly useful tool for identifying market reversals.

8.3 The Crab Pattern

The Crab pattern, presented by Scott Carney, also resembles a W-M setup but with different Fibonacci retracement points and an elongated form. Here's the rundown of the pattern:

- The XA leg retraces back approximately 38.2%, which forms point B.
- The AB leg retraces back approximately 88.6%, which forms point C.
- The BC leg retraces back approximately 361.8%, which forms point D (the reversal area).
- Point D must also be the approximately 161.8% retracement of the XA leg.

The pattern is named after its resemblance to the shape of a moving crab. Figure 8.8 provides a theoretical illustration of the Crab pattern.

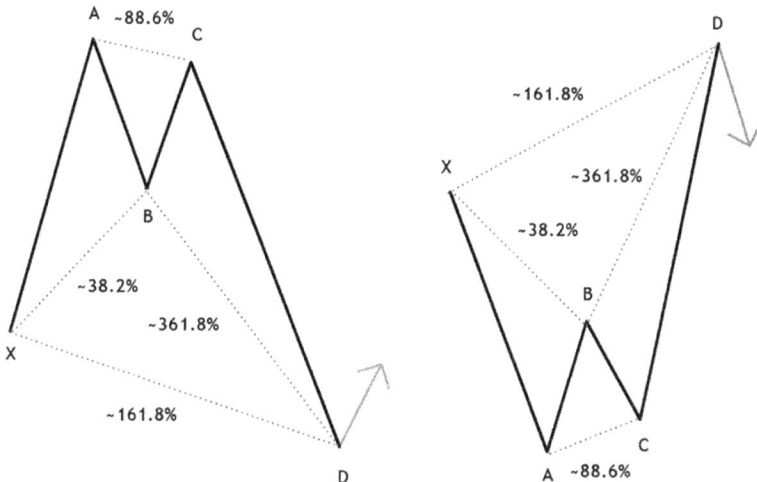

Figure 8.8 Crab pattern

The Crab pattern is purely complex, as there is no embedded ABCD pattern in it. Use the following function to detect Crab patterns.

```python
def detect_crab_pattern(my_time_series, swing_lookback=20, fib_tolerance=3):
  my_time_series['bullish_signal'] = 0
  my_time_series['bearish_signal'] = 0
  my_time_series = swing_detect(my_time_series, swing_lookback=swing_lookback)
  swings = []
  for idx, row in my_time_series.iterrows():
    if not pd.isna(row['swing_high']):
      swings.append((idx, 'high', row['swing_high']))
    elif not pd.isna(row['swing_low']):
      swings.append((idx, 'low', row['swing_low']))
  for i in range(len(swings)-4):
    p0, p1, p2, p3, p4 = swings[i:i+5]
    idx_x, type_x, px = p0
    idx_a, type_a, pa = p1
    idx_b, type_b, pb = p2
    idx_c, type_c, pc = p3
    idx_d, type_d, pd_ = p4
    if [type_x, type_a, type_b, type_c, type_d] == ['low', 'high', 'low', 'high', 'low']:
      xa = pa - px
      ab = pb - pa
      bc = pc - pb
      cd = pd_ - pc
      ad = pd_ - px
      if np.isclose(abs(ab) / abs(xa), 0.382, atol=fib_tolerance) and \
         0.382 <= abs(bc) / abs(ab) <= 0.886 and \
         1.618 <= abs(cd) / abs(bc) <= 3.618 and \
         np.isclose(abs(ad) / abs(xa), 1.618, atol=fib_tolerance) and \
         pd_ <= px:
        my_time_series.loc[idx_d+1, 'bullish_signal'] = 1
    elif [type_x, type_a, type_b, type_c, type_d] == ['high', 'low', 'high', 'low', 'high']:
      xa = px - pa
      ab = pa - pb
      bc = pb - pc
      cd = pc - pd_
      ad = px - pd_
      if np.isclose(abs(ab) / abs(xa), 0.382, atol=fib_tolerance) and \
         0.382 <= abs(bc) / abs(ab) <= 0.886 and \
         1.618 <= abs(cd) / abs(bc) <= 3.618 and \
         np.isclose(abs(ad) / abs(xa), 1.618, atol=fib_tolerance) and \
         pd_ >= px:
        my_time_series.loc[idx_d+1, 'bearish_signal'] = 1
  return my_time_series
```

Figure 8.9 shows a few detected signals from the function.

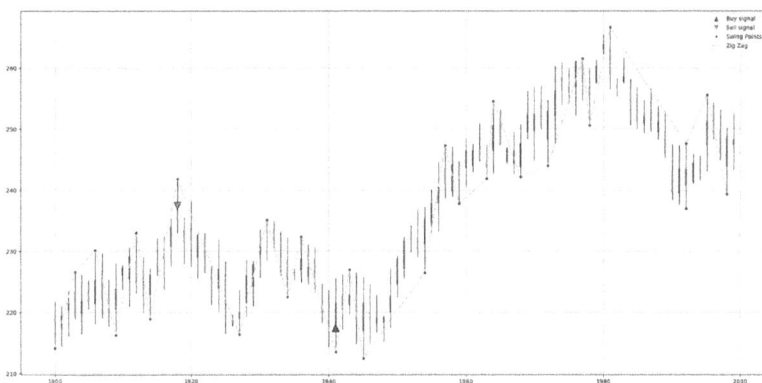

Figure 8.9 A signal chart showing a bearish and a bullish Crab pattern

Figure 8.10 shows a bearish Crab pattern.

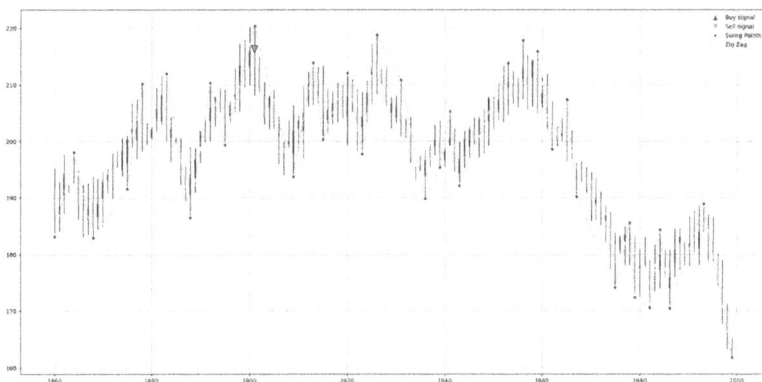

Figure 8.10 A signal chart showing a bearish Crab pattern

The Failed Extreme Impulsive Wave

The Failed Extreme Impulsive Wave (FEIW) is a unique harmonic pattern variation introduced by Scott Carney. It focuses on structures that initially resemble potential reversals but ultimately break down into strong trend continuations, often in a dramatic and impulsive manner. This pattern captures market behavior where price action overshoots traditional harmonic reversal zones, indicating a failure of expected mean reversion and instead suggesting continuation in the trend's direction. Here's the rundown of the pattern:

- The XA leg retraces back approximately 113% to 161.8%, which forms point B.
- The AB leg retraces back approximately 161.8% to 224%, which forms point C (the reversal area).

Figure 8.11 provides a theoretical illustration of FEIW.

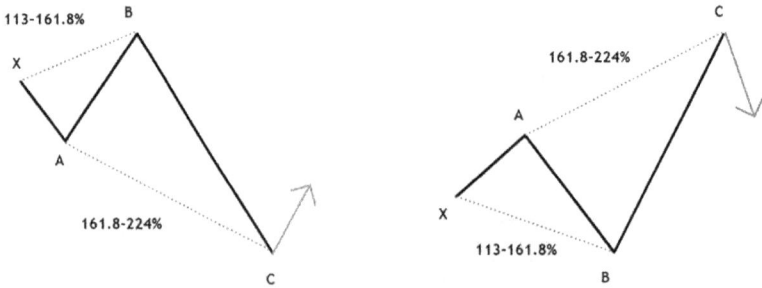

Figure 8.11 Failed extreme impulsive wave pattern

Figure 8.12 shows detected FEIW patterns.

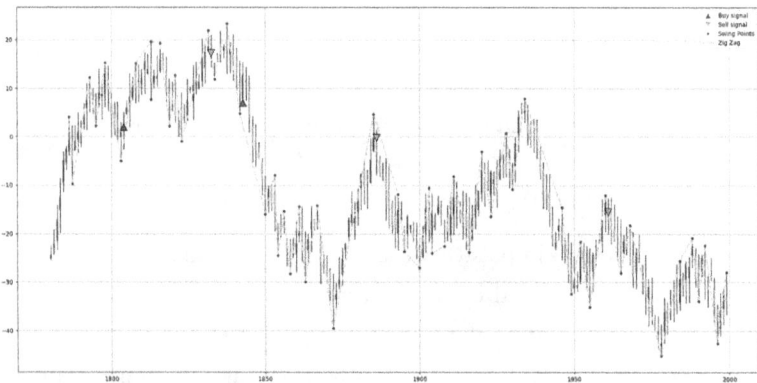

Figure 8.12 Signal chart showing detected FEIW patterns

What makes FEIW valuable is that it filters out premature reversal entries and instead highlights situations where aggressive price extension signals that the trend still has fuel. Traders use it to identify strong break-out setups in markets where traditional harmonic reversal patterns would be invalidated by excessive price momentum.

Harmonic Potential and Invalidation

The harmonic potential is the target area following a harmonic reaction from the reversal zone. It offers a basic guide as to where a trader may place their profit orders in case of pure harmonic trading. On the other hand, the harmonic invalidation is the threshold where the pattern is invalidated and is said to have failed to deliver a reaction (also known as a stop-loss). The expected reaction of harmonic patterns can be set in two ways:

- The Fibonacci method is used to set the potential and, to a lesser extent, the invalidation.
- The ATR way is used to set the potential and the invalidation of the pattern.

Harmonic potential and invalidation are basically risk management techniques to ensure a firsthand optimization of harmonic trading. Risk management in trading refers to the process of identifying, assessing, and mitigating the potential risks associated with trading activities. The goal of risk management is to limit the losses that can occur from trading while also maximizing potential profits. Let's start with the Fibonacci ratio way. Simply put, you can calculate the potential (target) of a harmonic pattern by retracing its two extreme points (highs and lows) and retaining two ratios: 38.2% as a first target and 61.8% as a second target. For example, to calculate the potential of an ABCD pattern, you would need to retrace from point A to point D. Then, you may target 38.2% of the move as a level from where you exit the position at a gain. This process is the same for other harmonic patterns. The Fibonacci ratio way is simple but may have drawbacks from time to time, such as the target being either very far or very close to the entry price, depending on the past price action. The second way entails the use of the ATR. Remember, it is the average fluctuations of points for a given period of time and therefore, you can use its values as multiple of stops and targets. Consider the two following examples:

- Trader A wants to buy a stock at $100 with a 14-period ATR of $10. She wants to use two times the ATR as a target and one time the ATR as a stop. Therefore, she places her target at $120 and her stop at $90. Trader A is risking $10 to gain $20, which is good risk management (refer to Chapter 12 for more information about the risk-reward ratio).
- Trader B wants to buy a stock at $50 with a 14-period ATR of $2. He wants to use two times the ATR as a target and three times the ATR as a stop. Therefore, he places his target at $54 and his stop at $44. Trader B is risking $6 to gain $4, which is suboptimal risk management.

These rules of thumb were created to facilitate harmonic trading, but it is ultimately up to you to create your risk management system.

CHAPTER 9

Pattern Recognition in Python III—Timing Patterns

Timing patterns are a special breed of market configurations that have time and price as variables. This means that, contrary to harmonic and candlestick patterns, which require only price, timing patterns require a time condition. This chapter discusses key timing patterns that add value to the overall trading framework and serve as an add-on to help raise the conviction of your ideas. A healthy trading framework must be composed of elements in the following nonexhaustive list:

- A fundamental (economic) idea on the asset you want to trade. This relates to the logical intuition as to why a certain asset should go up or down in the future. The fundamental idea can range from a basic expectation of a low-interest-rate environment (favoring the equities universe) to a complex balance sheet and demand analysis. In the short term, this type of idea is more complex and is reduced to news analysis, economic releases, and political shocks.
- A technical idea that analyzes the aggregate trend, the strength of the momentum, the signals from the indicators (e.g., the RSI), the patterns (e.g., timing patterns), and any anomalies that seem to corroborate the fundamental idea. It is crucial not to fall into the trap of confirmation bias. This type of bias makes you only look for elements that agree with your initial idea and disregard any other elements that are in conflict with this idea.
- A knowledge of the current market sentiment (pulse). The best traders out there analyze market sentiment in addition to fundamental and technical analysis. Sentiment analysis is out of this book's scope, but it is extremely important in understanding market drivers. Key sentiment indicators can include the put-call ratio and the Commitment of Traders (COT) report.

Tom DeMark's Sequential: The Setup

Tom DeMark (TD) is a well-known figure in the world of technical analysis. He has developed a range of proprietary indicators that aim to identify market trends and potential reversals. The TD setup is one of DeMark's foundational patterns used to identify a trend and its potential exhaustion point. It is a part of the broader TD sequential indicator, which includes more than just the setup. We will discuss the setup configuration in this book:

- A bullish setup requires nine consecutive closes each lower than the close four bars earlier.
- A bearish setup requires nine consecutive closes each higher than the close four bars earlier.

If a setup count reaches nine, it signals that the trend might be exhausted, and a potential reversal is expected. Figure 9.1 is a simplified theoretical illustration of the pattern.

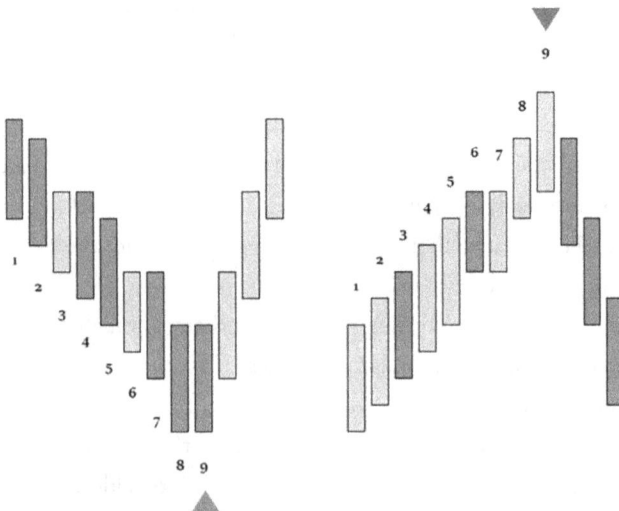

Figure 9.1 A theoretical illustration of the TD setup

The TD setup can come in two ways:

- A perfected TD setup where the low of bars 8 or 9 in the setup sequence must be less than the lows of bars 6 and 7 in the case of a bullish setup. On the other hand, for the bearish setup to be perfected, the high of bars 8 or 9 in the setup sequence must be greater than the highs of bars 6 and 7.
- An unperfected TD setup where the conditions relating to bars 8 and 9 seen in the previous point are not taken into account. Theoretically, perfected setups are preferred. In practice, I have found that results are mixed between the two. You will get the chance to back-test this in Chapter 12.

In reality, the TD setup pattern thrives during ranging markets (perfected or unperfected) and underperforms during trending markets. However, the last information doesn't necessarily have to be true, as using it correctly during a trending market can yield superior performance. By now, you should understand that this is a reversal timing pattern, which means the following:

- During a bullish market, only look for TD bullish setups, which occur during small market corrections within the overall bullish trend.
- During a bearish market, only look for TD bearish setups, which occur during small market recoveries within the overall bearish trend.

The code block for the TD setup is lengthy and can be found in the GitHub repository. The argument **perfect** can be set to **True** if you only want to detect perfected patterns; otherwise, the default argument is **False**. Figure 9.2 shows a few perfected signals generated by the code.

Figure 9.2 A signal chart showing TD signals

In conclusion, the TD setup is a simple pattern worth looking at, especially during ranging markets. Its main aim is to confirm any directional ideas and provide a timing factor. As an important disclaimer, I have neither affiliation with TD nor do I endorse his indicators. I simply share his publicly available indicator while giving him full credit and giving my own personal opinion on them.

The Fibonacci Timing Pattern

Inspired by the TD setup pattern, the Fibonacci timing pattern is a timing tool I've developed to catch short-term reversals. It uses Fibonacci numbers as time variables. The algorithmic intuition is the same as the TD setup, but has the following conditions:

- A bullish Fibonacci timing pattern requires eight consecutive closes where each close is below the close from five periods ago and the close from five periods ago is below the close from 21 periods ago as of the close from five periods ago.
- A bearish Fibonacci timing pattern requires eight consecutive closes where each close is above the close from five periods ago and the close from five periods ago is above the close from 21 periods ago as of the close from five periods ago.

The following code shows the function of the Fibonacci timing pattern.

```
def fibonacci_timing_pattern(my_time_series, source='close', final_step=8, first_difference=5,
second_difference=21):
    my_time_series['buy_setup'] = 0
    my_time_series['sell_setup'] = 0
    my_time_series['bullish_signal'] = 0
    my_time_series['bearish_signal'] = 0
    for i in range(0, len(my_time_series)):
        # bullish setup
        if my_time_series[source].iloc[i] < my_time_series[source].iloc[i - first_difference] and \
            my_time_series[source].iloc[i - first_difference] < my_time_series[source].iloc[i -
                                second_difference]:
            my_time_series.at[my_time_series.index[i], 'buy_setup'] = my_time_series['buy_setup'].iloc[i - 1] + 1
if my_time_series['buy_setup'].iloc[i - 1] < final_step else 0
        else:
            my_time_series.at[my_time_series.index[i], 'buy_setup'] = 0
        # bearish setup
        if my_time_series[source].iloc[i] > my_time_series[source].iloc[i - first_difference] and \
            my_time_series[source].iloc[i - first_difference] > my_time_series[source].iloc[i -
                                second_difference]:
            my_time_series.at[my_time_series.index[i], 'sell_setup'] = my_time_series['sell_setup'].iloc[i - 1] + 1
if my_time_series['sell_setup'].iloc[i - 1] < final_step else 0
        else:
            my_time_series.at[my_time_series.index[i], 'sell_setup'] = 0
    for i in range(0, len(my_time_series)):
        try:
            if my_time_series['buy_setup'].iloc[i] == final_step:
                my_time_series['bullish_signal'].iloc[i+1] = 1
            elif my_time_series['sell_setup'].iloc[i] == final_step:
                my_time_series['bearish_signal'].iloc[i+1] = 1
        except (KeyError, IndexError):
            pass
    return my_time_series
```

Figure 9.3 shows a signal chart with the Fibonacci timing pattern.

Figure 9.3 A signal chart showing Fibonacci timing pattern signals

The pattern can be used in tandem with the TD setup pattern. You can also create a scorecard that records instances where multiple patterns occur around a certain zone, and see how the reaction of the market will be after that. I call this technique swarming, and it's where you use a number of indicators and patterns to see where they point to the most. This allows you to confirm a strong reactionary zone.

Combining Patterns with Alternative Charts

I have noticed that most of the time, the application of timing patterns to alternative charts, such as Heikin-Ashi and K's candlesticks, yields a superior predictive quality or, at the very least, an alternative picture from conventional techniques. As the two alternative charting systems have less noise than standard candlestick charts, timing patterns could be better detected. To do this experiment, you can simply apply the functions k_candlesticks() and heikin_ashi() on the time series and then use the td_setup() function as follows.

Figure 9.4 shows a signal chart of the TD setup when applied to Heikin-Ashi. The chart shows the signal superimposed on the regular bar chart.

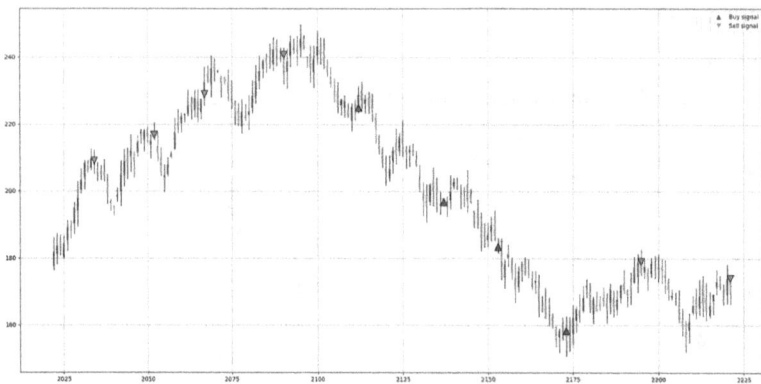

Figure 9.4 Applying pattern recognition tools to Heikin-Ashi charts

Figure 9.5 shows the signal chart of the TD setup when applied to K's CCS. The chart shows the signal superimposed on the regular bar chart.

Figure 9.5 Applying pattern recognition tools to K's CCS

The interesting part is where you consider the signal only when it's visible across all three candlestick systems. This gives it more weight, albeit at the cost of the frequency. In summary, this chapter presented a few timing patterns and the logic behind them. Additionally, you have seen that you can apply these patterns to other types of candlestick charts in order to have another angle.

## CHAPTER 10

Pattern Recognition in Python IV—Price Patterns

Classic technical analysis teaches that there are visible price patterns that may point to a possible known outcome. Among these patterns are double tops/bottoms and head and shoulders patterns. This chapter shows how to detect and code these classic technical analysis price patterns.

Double Top and Double Bottom Patterns

Double top and double bottom patterns are used to identify potential reversals in market trends. These patterns are formed by the price movement of an asset and are generally considered adequate indicators of trend reversals when confirmed. We can define both patterns as follows:

- A double bottom is a bullish reversal pattern that forms at the end of a downtrend. It is characterized by two distinct troughs (bottoms) at approximately the same price level, with a moderate peak (ridge) in between. The pattern is confirmed when the price rises above the level of the peak after the second bottom. This level is known as the bullish neckline.
- A double bottom is a bearish reversal pattern that forms at the end of an uptrend. It is characterized by two distinct peaks (tops) at approximately the same price level, with a moderate trough (valley) in between. The pattern is confirmed when the price falls below the level of the trough after the second top. This level is known as the bearish neckline.

The following theoretical illustration shows a double bottom and a double top (Figure 10.1).

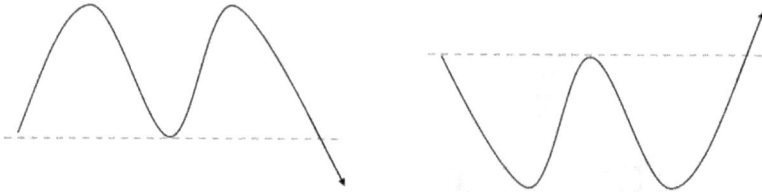

Figure 10.1 **A theoretical illustration of a double top** (left) **and a double bottom** (right)

The double bottom suggests that the asset is finding support at a certain level. Once the neckline is surpassed, it often indicates a reversal from a downtrend to an uptrend. The double top suggests that the asset is finding resistance at a certain level. Once the neckline is broken, it often indicates a reversal from an uptrend to a downtrend. Ideally, the two tops or bottoms should be symmetrical, but this is rarely the case in real life. The pattern can also form over various timeframes, from intraday to weekly charts. Volume typically declines during the formation of the pattern and increases upon the breakout of the neckline. Use the following code to create the algorithm that detects double bottoms and double tops given OHLC data frames.

```
def detect_double_top_bottom(my_time_series, swing_lookback=20,
tolerance=0.05):
  my_time_series['bullish_signal'] = 0
  my_time_series['bearish_signal'] = 0
  swings = []
  my_time_series = swing_detect(my_time_series,
swing_lookback=swing_lookback)
  for idx, row in my_time_series.iterrows():
    if not pd.isna(row['swing_low']):
      swings.append((idx, 'low', row['swing_low']))
    elif not pd.isna(row['swing_high']):
      swings.append((idx, 'high', row['swing_high']))
  for i in range(len(swings) - 2):
    idx1, type1, val1 = swings[i]
    idx2, type2, val2 = swings[i+1]
    idx3, type3, val3 = swings[i+2]
    if type1 == 'low' and type2 == 'high' and type3 == 'low':
      if val3 >= val1 and val3 <= val1 * (1 + tolerance):
```

```
        neckline = val2
        for j in range(idx3 + 1, len(my_time_series)):
          if not pd.isna(my_time_series.loc[j, 'swing_low']):
            break
          elif my_time_series.loc[j, 'close'] > neckline:
            my_time_series.loc[j+1, 'bullish_signal'] = 1
            break
  for idx, row in my_time_series.iterrows():
    if not pd.isna(row['swing_high']):
      swings.append((idx, 'high', row['swing_high']))
    elif not pd.isna(row['swing_low']):
      swings.append((idx, 'low', row['swing_low']))
  for i in range(len(swings) - 2):
    idx1, type1, val1 = swings[i]
    idx2, type2, val2 = swings[i+1]
    idx3, type3, val3 = swings[i+2]
    if type1 == 'high' and type2 == 'low' and type3 == 'high':
      if val3 <= val1 and val3 >= val1 * (1 - tolerance):
        neckline = val2  # the swing low between the tops
        for j in range(idx3 + 1, len(my_time_series)):
          if not pd.isna(my_time_series.loc[j, 'swing_high']):
            break
          elif my_time_series.loc[j, 'close'] < neckline:
            my_time_series.loc[j+1, 'bearish_signal'] = 1
            break
  return my_time_series
```

Figure 10.2 shows a double bottom detected by the algorithm.

Figure 10.2 A signal chart detecting a double bottom

Figure 10.3 shows a double top detected by the algorithm.

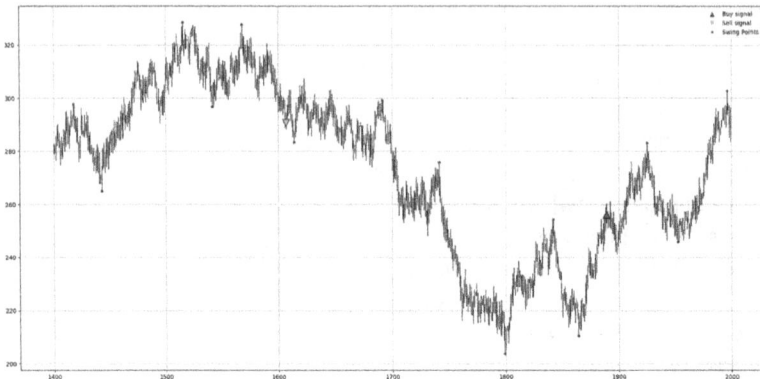

Figure 10.3 A signal chart detecting a double top

Even with the technological advancements in the world of trading, classic simple patterns still find their place in analysis. Having worked as a professional technical analyst dealing with institutional players, I can guarantee that everyone looks at such patterns to find opportunities.

The Head and Shoulders Pattern

The head and shoulders pattern is another chart pattern used to identify reversals in market trends:

- An inverse head and shoulders is a bullish reversal pattern that forms at the end of a downtrend. It is characterized by three troughs: a lower trough (head) between two higher troughs (shoulders). The neckline is drawn by connecting the highest points of the peaks between the shoulders and the head. It can be horizontal or slanted. The pattern is confirmed when the price breaks above the neckline after forming the right shoulder.
- A head and shoulders is a bearish reversal pattern that forms at the end of an uptrend. It is characterized by three peaks: a higher peak (head) between two lower peaks (shoulders). The neckline is drawn by connecting the lowest points of the troughs between the shoulders and the head. It can be horizontal or slanted. The pattern is confirmed when the price breaks below the neckline after forming the right shoulder.

The head and shoulders pattern suggests that the asset is unable to maintain its uptrend. A break below the neckline often indicates a reversal from an uptrend to a downtrend. The inverse head and shoulders pattern suggests that the asset is unable to maintain its downtrend. A break above the neckline often indicates a reversal from a downtrend to an uptrend. The following theoretical illustration shows a head and shoulders and an inverted head and shoulders pattern (Figure 10.4).

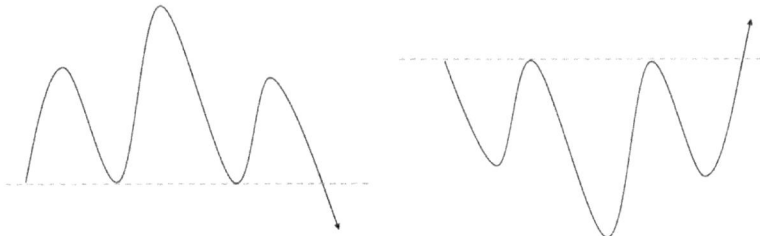

Figure 10.4 *A theoretical illustration of a head and shoulders* (left) *and an inverse head and shoulders* (right)

The code of this pattern can be found in the GitHub repository.

The head and shoulders pattern remains one of the pillars of technical analysis, as throughout time, it has been seen around major market reversals. Figure 10.5 shows a head and shoulders pattern detected right before an inverse head and shoulders pattern.

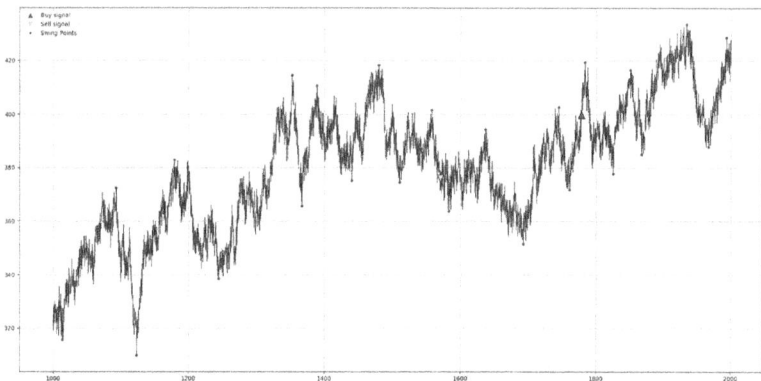

Figure 10.5 *A signal chart with detected head and shoulders patterns within a bullish trend*

Figure 10.6 shows a head and shoulders pattern.

Figure 10.6 *A signal chart with detected head and shoulders patterns within a bearish trend*

The Gap Pattern

Gap patterns refer to areas on a price chart where the price of a security moves sharply up or down with no trading in between. As a result, the chart shows a void in the price series. Think of it as the price going from $100 to $102 without passing through $101. The following theoretical illustration shows a gap up and a gap down (Figure 10.7).

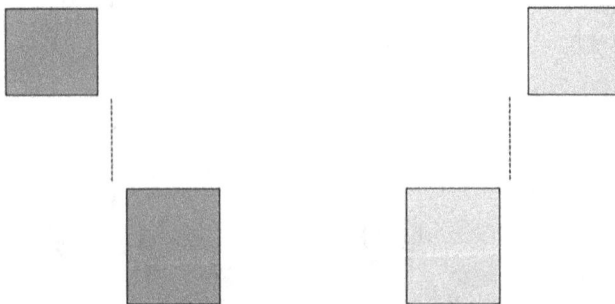

Figure 10.7 *Gap pattern*

There are a few different types of gaps:

- A breakaway gap occurs at the beginning of a trend, signaling a strong shift in market sentiment. Breakaway gaps often follow a period of consolidation or a congestion area.

- A runaway gap appears in the middle of a trend and indicates strong interest in continuing the trend. They are often accompanied by increased volume.
- An exhaustion gap occurs near the end of a trend and can signal a final push before the trend reverses. They are typically followed by a sharp reversal.
- A common gap is often not significant and can occur frequently. They typically happen in normal market conditions. The ideal common gap appears during a ranging (sideways) market, and is traded using a technique referred to as filling the gap.

There is no reliable way to know which type of gap is occurring; this is why the classification of gaps is not possible a priori. After a common gap, prices typically return to the level before the gap, and this is referred to as filling the gap. This can happen due to profit-taking, corrections, or reassessment of the gap's significance. Breakaway and runaway gaps may remain unfilled for extended periods or indefinitely. This is why we will focus on common gaps and develop a contrarian mindset upon detecting them. Not all gaps indicate a true change in trend. Some gaps might be short-lived and can lead to false signals. Let's now code a function that seeks out gaps and emits contrarian signals if the conditions are met. Algorithmically, we want to do the following:

- Find instances where the open price is below the previous close price. This signals a gap down, and thus a bullish opportunity to fill the gap through a recovery.
- Find instances where the open price is above the previous close price. This signals a gap up, and thus a bearish opportunity to fill the gap through a correction.

However, it is important to know the minimum size of the gap. Not every gap is worth trading. For example, is a 0.0001 (one pip) gap on NZDUSD worth entering, knowing that the spread is at least 0.0003 (three pips) for most retail traders? Clearly not. So, how do we determine the minimum size automatically? We can use a volatility multiplier as a minimum value of a gap (all the while being aware of the transaction costs incurred during each trade):

- Calculate a 14-period ATR to approximate the current market volatility.
- Whenever a gap occurs, check the most recent ATR value. If the gap's distance is greater than the value of the ATR plus a margin for transaction costs, then the gap is tradable.
- You have to target the level that fills the gap. With a bullish or a bearish signal, you should put the previous close price as the target (a more conservative way is to target the previous low in a bullish position and the previous high in a bearish position).

The following code block shows the algorithm in action.

```python
def gap(my_time_series, atr_column, min_size):
    my_time_series['bullish_signal'] = 0
    my_time_series['bearish_signal'] = 0
    my_time_series = atr(my_time_series)
    for i in range(0, len(my_time_series)):
        # bullish gap
        if my_time_series['open'].iloc[i] < my_time_series['close'].iloc[i - 1] and \
            (my_time_series['close'].iloc[i - 1] - my_time_series['open'].iloc[i]) > \
            (my_time_series['volatility'].iloc[i - 1] * min_size):
            my_time_series.at[my_time_series.index[i], 'bullish_signal'] = 1
        # bearish gap
        elif my_time_series['open'].iloc[i] > my_time_series['close'].iloc[i - 1] and \
            (my_time_series['open'].iloc[i] - my_time_series['close'].iloc[i - 1]) > \
            (my_time_series['volatility'].iloc[i - 1] * min_size):
            my_time_series.at[my_time_series.index[i], 'bearish_signal'] = 1
    return my_time_series
```

Remember, the code is saved in the GitHub repository; you only need to download the files and run them. Let's take a look at a few signals generated by the algorithm (Figure 10.8).

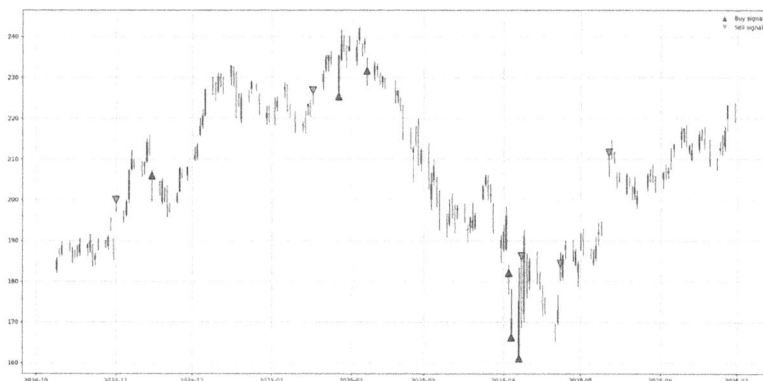

Figure 10.8 A signal chart with detected gap patterns

Trading gaps can be particularly challenging for several reasons, especially when factoring in the discrepancies between different brokers. One of the most frustrating aspects of trading gaps is that not all brokers display the same price data. This stems from the fact that each broker may use a different set of banks or liquidity pools, leading to slightly different bid/ask prices. Additionally, the open/close time of candles or sessions can vary depending on broker time zone settings, which can make a gap visible on one platform but not another. Also, some brokers may smooth out price data or filter out extreme ticks, causing a gap to appear smaller or even invisible.

In summary, classic price patterns still have their place in current markets. It's important to devise clear rules in order to eliminate the subjectivity they carry. This way, it becomes simpler to back-test them in order to understand their efficacy and profitability.

CHAPTER 11

A New Breed of Technical Indicators

This chapter presents the best indicators from my personal library of indicators—*K's collection*—that I have developed over the years with the aim of diversifying and improving the market predictive capabilities. K's collection is different from the rainbow indicators presented in Chapter 3 in the sense that the indicators of the former are more sophisticated, while the latter can mostly be considered as techniques applied to indicators. Classic technical indicators like moving averages remain, by default, the most monitored by traders, and thus, potentially have a stronger market impact in case they show a clear configuration. Nevertheless, modern indicators, especially the ones from K's collection, seek to improve classic technical analysis by combining indicators or by using new techniques to forecast market reactions and deliver a useful piece of information about the market's state. Each section of this chapter will present an indicator from K's collection.

K's Reversal Indicator I

This indicator will give us the chance to discuss a popular classic technical indicator before we present it. K's reversal indicator I is composed of Bollinger bands and the moving average convergence divergence (MACD) oscillator. The MACD is a classic technical indicator used to identify changes in the strength and direction of a trend. It consists of three components:

- MACD line: This is the difference between a 12-period EMA and a 26-period EMA.
- Signal line: This is a 9-period EMA applied to the MACD line.
- Histogram: This is the difference between the MACD line and the signal line.

Crossovers between the MACD line and signal line are the most common signals watched. Use the following code to create the MACD given an OHLC data frame.

```
def macd(my_time_series, source='close', short_window=12, long_window=26, signal_window=9):
    # calculate the short-term EMA
    my_time_series['EMA_short'] = my_time_series[source].ewm(span=short_window,
                                    adjust=False).mean()
    # calculate the long-term EMA
    my_time_series['EMA_long'] = my_time_series[source].ewm(span=long_window, adjust=False).mean()
    # calculate the MACD line
    my_time_series['MACD_line'] = my_time_series['EMA_short'] - my_time_series['EMA_long']
    # calculate the Signal line
    my_time_series['MACD_signal'] = my_time_series['MACD_line'].ewm(span=signal_window,
                                    adjust=False).mean()
    # calculate the MACD Histogram
    my_time_series['MACD_histogram'] = my_time_series['MACD_line'] - my_time_series['MACD_signal']
    # drop the EMA columns as they are not needed anymore
    my_time_series.drop(['EMA_short', 'EMA_long'], axis=1, inplace=True)
    return my_time_series.dropna()
```

Figure 11.1 shows how the MACD looks with respect to the time series it represents.

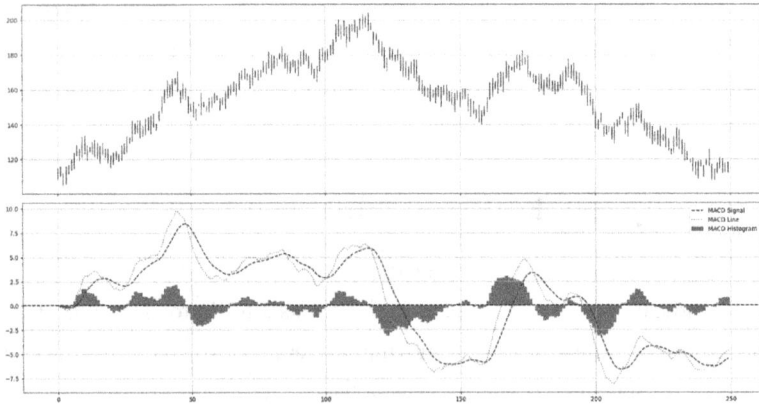

Figure 11.1 **MACD**

The MACD can be used as a trend-following indicator. When the MACD line crosses above the signal line, it generates a bullish signal, suggesting upward momentum. When the MACD line crosses below the signal line, it generates a bearish signal, suggesting downward momentum. Similarly, when the MACD line crosses above the zero line, it suggests upward momentum, and when it crosses below the zero line, it signals a shift toward downward momentum. Let's go back to the discussion on K's reversal indicator I. The signals are found through a combination of the MACD and Bollinger bands. Here's how:

- A bullish signal is generated whenever the smaller value between the open and close price is below the 100-period lower Bollinger band. Simultaneously, the MACD line must cross over the MACD signal.
- A bearish signal is generated whenever the larger value between the open and close price is above the 100-period upper Bollinger band. Simultaneously, the MACD line must cross under the MACD signal.

Therefore, in simple terms, the signal is given by combining a reversal indicator (Bollinger bands) with a trend-following technique (the MACD signal lines cross). This is a hybrid technique that has the potential to yield very interesting directional signals. The bullish signal is found by an extremely oversold condition with the market price below the lower Bollinger band, combined with a bullish continuation confirmation stemming from the MACD line. In parallel, the bearish signal is found by an extremely overbought condition with the market price above the upper Bollinger band, combined with a bearish continuation confirmation stemming from the MACD line. The following code block shows how to define K's reversal indicator I.

```
def k_reversal_indicator_I(my_time_series):
  my_time_series = macd(my_time_series, source='close', short_window=12, long_window=26, signal_window=9)
  my_time_series = bollinger_bands(my_time_series, source='close', bb_lookback=100, num_std_dev=2)
  my_time_series['bullish_signal'] = 0
  my_time_series['bearish_signal'] = 0
  for i in range(0, len(my_time_series)):
    # bullish signal
    if my_time_series['low'].iloc[i] < my_time_series['lower_band'].iloc[i] and \
      my_time_series['high'].iloc[i] < my_time_series['middle_band'].iloc[i] and \
      my_time_series['MACD_line'].iloc[i] > my_time_series['MACD_signal'].iloc[i] and \
      my_time_series['MACD_line'].iloc[i-1] < my_time_series['MACD_signal'].iloc[i-1]:
      my_time_series.at[my_time_series.index[i+1], 'bullish_signal'] = 1
    # bearish signal
    elif my_time_series['high'].iloc[i] > my_time_series['upper_band'].iloc[i] and \
      my_time_series['low'].iloc[i] > my_time_series['middle_band'].iloc[i] and \
      my_time_series['MACD_line'].iloc[i] < my_time_series['MACD_signal'].iloc[i] and \
      my_time_series['MACD_line'].iloc[i-1] > my_time_series['MACD_signal'].iloc[i-1]:
      my_time_series.at[my_time_series.index[i+1], 'bearish_signal'] = 1
  return my_time_series
```

Figure 11.2 shows a few signals generated by the indicator.

Figure 11.2 A signal chart showing K's reversal indicator I

The best practices to follow while using this indicator are as follows:

- Ideally, as with any reversal indicator (classic or modern), it is best used during a sideways market. This ensures that the balance between supply and demand favors more precision.
- The indicator has an inherent confirmation factor in it, which is the MACD crossing over or under the signal line; therefore, there is no need for an extra filter to validate the signals.
- The lookback periods of the indicator are the result of a large number of experiments and are theoretically suitable for all types of time series. Therefore, even though you are encouraged to tweak the parameters (e.g., change the 100-period lookback), it is important to consider that it is the result of a generalized optimization effort.

In conclusion, K's reversal indicator I is a powerful reversal tool in modern technical analysis. It combines the strengths of Bollinger bands and the MACD to predict market inflections.

K's Reversal Indicator II

If I have to select a favorite among all the indicators of K's collection, then my choice goes to K's reversal indicator II. This does not in any way compromise the quality of the other indicators, but simply points to how well this indicator does a good job of determining local tops and bottoms. K's reversal indicator II has no relation whatsoever to K's reversal indicator I, as it is based on a combination of price, time, and mean reversion. Let's see how to develop this indicator:

1. Calculate a moving average (by default, a 13-period moving average).
2. Calculate the number of times the market is above its moving average. Whenever that number hits 21, a bearish signal is generated, and whenever that number hits zero, a bullish signal is generated.

The following code block shows how to define K's reversal indicator II.

```python
def k_reversal_indicator_I(my_time_series):
    my_time_series = macd(my_time_series, source='close', short_window=12, long_window=26, signal_window=9)
    my_time_series = bollinger_bands(my_time_series, source='close', bb_lookback=100, num_std_dev=2)
    my_time_series['bullish_signal'] = 0
    my_time_series['bearish_signal'] = 0
    for i in range(0, len(my_time_series)):
        # bullish signal
        if my_time_series['low'].iloc[i] < my_time_series['lower_band'].iloc[i] and \
            my_time_series['high'].iloc[i] < my_time_series['middle_band'].iloc[i] and \
            my_time_series['MACD_line'].iloc[i] > my_time_series['MACD_signal'].iloc[i] and \
            my_time_series['MACD_line'].iloc[i-1] < my_time_series['MACD_signal'].iloc[i-1]:
                my_time_series.at[my_time_series.index[i+1], 'bullish_signal'] = 1
        # bearish signal
        elif my_time_series['high'].iloc[i] > my_time_series['upper_band'].iloc[i] and \
            my_time_series['low'].iloc[i] > my_time_series['middle_band'].iloc[i] and \
            my_time_series['MACD_line'].iloc[i] < my_time_series['MACD_signal'].iloc[i] and \
            my_time_series['MACD_line'].iloc[i-1] > my_time_series['MACD_signal'].iloc[i-1]:
                my_time_series.at[my_time_series.index[i+1], 'bearish_signal'] = 1
    return my_time_series
```

Figure 11.3 shows a few signals generated by the indicator.

Figure 11.3 A signal chart showing K's reversal indicator II

You can see how this indicator has more frequent signals than its predecessor. This can be an advantage to opportunistic traders. The best practices to follow using this indicator are as follows:

- It is best used during a ranging (sideways) market for the same reasons mentioned previously in the section on K's reversal indicator I.
- The indicator takes as variables: time, price, and a price-derived calculation (SMA). It is therefore a three-dimensional measure that aims to detect hidden market maxima and minima. This means that it is quite possible to use it as a stand-alone indicator, something that is discouraged with other indicators.
- The lookback periods of the indicator are the result of a large number of experiments and are theoretically suitable for all types of time series. As with K's reversal indicator I, you can tweak the parameters, but keep in mind the default lookback periods.

In conclusion, K's reversal indicator II can be categorized as a market directional system as opposed to just an indicator. It is a prime example of modern technical analysis, which fuses three elements (time, price, and a price-derived indicator) in order to detect market reactions.

K's ATR-Adjusted RSI

It is worth asking what happens when we try to fuse volatility and momentum. For example, if we take the ATR and try to fuse it with the RSI, what would be the result? K's ATR-adjusted RSI answers this question by properly combining both indicators into one that detects reversals while taking into account volatility. Follow these steps to create the indicator:

1. Calculate a 13-period RSI on the close price.
2. Calculate a 5-period ATR on the OHLC data.
3. Multiply the RSI calculation from step 1 by the ATR calculation from step 2.
4. Calculate a 13-period RSI of the result from step 3.

Use the following code snippet to create the indicator's function.

```
def atr_adjusted_rsi(my_time_series, source='close', rsi_lookback=13, vol_lookback=5, rsi_atr_lookback=13):

  my_time_series = rsi(my_time_series, source='close', output_name='RSI', rsi_lookback=rsi_lookback)

  my_time_series = atr(my_time_series, vol_lookback=vol_lookback)

  my_time_series['RSI_times_atr'] = my_time_series['RSI'] * my_time_series['volatility']

  my_time_series = rsi(my_time_series, source='RSI_times_atr', output_name='atr_adjusted_rsi',
rsi_lookback=rsi_atr_lookback)

  return my_time_series.dropna()
```

Figure 11.4 shows the ATR-adjusted RSI in action.

Figure 11.4 ATR-adjusted RSI in action

It's worth noting that you should tweak the lookback period of both components (RSI and ATR) to find the optimal one for you. I have chosen 13 as the default after a few optimizations, but markets are dynamic and change properties constantly; therefore, you are encouraged to play around with the parameters.

K's RSI²

So far, you have been applying the RSI's formula to the close price. This means that the source value of the RSI is the time series' close price. But what if the source price of the RSI was the RSI itself? The RSI² (pronounced RSI square) is a simple indicator I've developed to predict the

RSI's future direction by using the divergence technique. The steps required to calculate the RSI² are as follows:

- Calculate a 14-period RSI with the source value set to the close price.
- Calculate a 5-period RSI with the source value set to the RSI from step 1.

By now, you should be familiar with how we code indicators. Therefore, the following code snippet should not be complicated to understand.

```
def rsi_square(my_time_series, source='close', rsi_prime_lookback=14, rsi_square_lookback=5):
    my_time_series = rsi(my_time_series, source=source, output_name='RSI',
                rsi_lookback=rsi_prime_lookback)
    my_time_series = rsi(my_time_series, source='RSI', output_name='RSI²',
                rsi_lookback=rsi_prime_lookback)
    return my_time_series.dropna()
```

Previously, with the Yellow indicator, you have seen the slope divergence technique. K's RSI² will give you a chance to fully understand the real divergence technique. Divergence is different from slope divergence, and it is a means to spot early signs of a possible change in the ongoing trend. Imagine you're walking uphill (price is going up), but you're getting more tired with each step (momentum is going down). At some point, you'll probably stop or turn around. That's divergence: the price is doing one thing (e.g., going higher), but the strength behind it (measured by indicators like the RSI or MACD) is doing the opposite. It often signals that the trend may soon reverse or slow down. There are two main types:

- Bullish divergence: Price makes lower lows, but the indicator makes higher lows. This indicates that the market might go up soon.
- Bearish divergence: Price makes higher highs, but the indicator makes lower highs. This indicates that the market might go down soon.

When RSI² is showing higher lows while the RSI is showing lower lows, a bullish divergence is confirmed. In contrast, when RSI² is showing lower highs while the RSI is showing higher highs, a bearish divergence is confirmed. The divergence technique plays on the strong correlation between the RSI and the underlying security price. The hypothesis is that if it's possible to forecast reversals in the RSI, then it may be possible to relate these reversals to the security's price. Figure 11.5 shows the RSI^2.

Figure 11.5 RSI^2 (dashed) versus regular RSI

Figure 11.6 shows divergence signals on RSI^2 versus RSI.

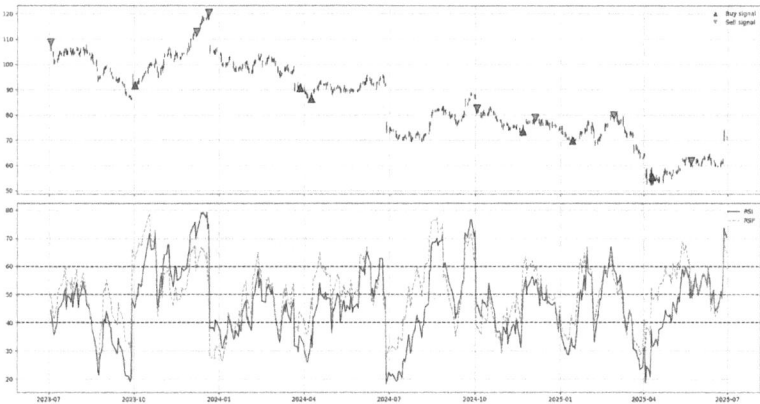

Figure 11.6 Divergence signals using RSI^2

Using the divergence technique on the RSI^2 adds a fresh new way to detect market exhaustion. Note that originally, the divergence is to be used on the RSI values directly as opposed to the RSI^2. You are encouraged to tweak the code slightly so that the divergence function is applied to the RSI.

K's MARSI

By now, you should understand what a moving average is. Additionally, you should also have a solid knowledge of the RSI. K's moving average RSI (MARSI) fuses the two together in the following way:

- Calculate a 20-period SMA on the close prices.
- Calculate a 14-period RSI on the values of the moving average calculated in step 1.

Use the following code to create the MARSI.

```python
def marsi(my_time_series, ma_lookback=200, rsi_lookback=20):
  my_time_series = moving_average(my_time_series, 'close',
ma_lookback=ma_lookback)
  my_time_series = rsi(my_time_series, 'moving_average', 'MARSI',
rsi_lookback=rsi_lookback)
  my_time_series['bullish_signal'] = 0
  my_time_series['bearish_signal'] = 0
  for i in range(0, len(my_time_series)):
    try:
      # bullish signal
      if my_time_series['MARSI'].iloc[i] > 2 and \
       my_time_series['MARSI'].iloc[i-1] < 2 and \
       my_time_series['MARSI'].iloc[i-2] < 2 and \
       my_time_series['MARSI'].iloc[i-3] < 2:
         my_time_series.at[my_time_series.index[i+1], 'bullish_signal'] = 1
      # bearish signal
      elif my_time_series['MARSI'].iloc[i] < 98 and \
       my_time_series['MARSI'].iloc[i-1] > 98 and \
       my_time_series['MARSI'].iloc[i-2] > 98 and \
       my_time_series['MARSI'].iloc[i-3] > 98:
         my_time_series.at[my_time_series.index[i+1], 'bearish_signal'] = 1
    except KeyError:
     pass
  return my_time_series
```

The default technique to use with the MARSI is the following:

- A bullish signal is generated whenever the MARSI surpasses 2 after spending at least two periods below it.
- A bearish signal is generated whenever the MARSI breaks 98 after spending at least two periods above it.

Note that you can adjust the parameters of the indicator to suit your type of trading. Figure 11.7 shows the different signals produced by K's MARSI. Notice its smoothness due to the fact that the RSI is applied on smoothed data (the 20-period SMA). This has the potential to clean out false signals, albeit at the cost of significant lag.

Figure 11.7 MARSI

K's MARSI helps confirm market reversals, but may have a lag factor in it, considering the conditions and the components of the indicator. I typically use MARSI in ranging markets.

K's Fibonacci Moving Average

K's Fibonacci moving average (FMA) is a type of SMMA calculated from Fibonacci lookback periods. Here's how:

- Calculate 15 EMAs, each having one of the following lookback periods {2, 3, 5, 8, 13, 21, 34, 55, 89, 144, 233, 377, 610, 987, 1597}.

- The calculation from the first step is to be done on the highs and on the lows.
- For each time step, take the simple average of the 15 EMAs for both highs and lows, thus creating a rolling zone of an average of 15 EMAs.

Use the following code to create the FMA.

```python
def fibonacci_moving_average(my_time_series):
    my_time_series['fma_high'] = (my_time_series['high'].ewm(span=2, adjust=False).mean() + \
            my_time_series['high'].ewm(span=3, adjust=False).mean() + \
            my_time_series['high'].ewm(span=5, adjust=False).mean() + \
            my_time_series['high'].ewm(span=8, adjust=False).mean() + \
            my_time_series['high'].ewm(span=13, adjust=False).mean() + \
            my_time_series['high'].ewm(span=21, adjust=False).mean() + \
            my_time_series['high'].ewm(span=34, adjust=False).mean() + \
            my_time_series['high'].ewm(span=55, adjust=False).mean() + \
            my_time_series['high'].ewm(span=89, adjust=False).mean() + \
            my_time_series['high'].ewm(span=144, adjust=False).mean() + \
            my_time_series['high'].ewm(span=233, adjust=False).mean() + \
            my_time_series['high'].ewm(span=377, adjust=False).mean() + \
            my_time_series['high'].ewm(span=610, adjust=False).mean() + \
            my_time_series['high'].ewm(span=987, adjust=False).mean() + \
            my_time_series['high'].ewm(span=1597, adjust=False).mean()) / 15
    my_time_series['fma_low'] = (my_time_series['low'].ewm(span=2, adjust=False).mean() + \
            my_time_series['low'].ewm(span=3, adjust=False).mean() + \
            my_time_series['low'].ewm(span=5, adjust=False).mean() + \
            my_time_series['low'].ewm(span=8, adjust=False).mean() + \
            my_time_series['low'].ewm(span=13, adjust=False).mean() + \
            my_time_series['low'].ewm(span=21, adjust=False).mean() + \
            my_time_series['low'].ewm(span=34, adjust=False).mean() + \
            my_time_series['low'].ewm(span=55, adjust=False).mean() + \
            my_time_series['low'].ewm(span=89, adjust=False).mean() + \
            my_time_series['low'].ewm(span=144, adjust=False).mean() + \
            my_time_series['low'].ewm(span=233, adjust=False).mean() + \
            my_time_series['low'].ewm(span=377, adjust=False).mean() + \
            my_time_series['low'].ewm(span=610, adjust=False).mean() + \
            my_time_series['low'].ewm(span=987, adjust=False).mean() + \
            my_time_series['low'].ewm(span=1597, adjust=False).mean()) / 15
    return my_time_series.dropna()
```

Figure 11.8 shows the FMA in action. Its main use is to provide dynamic support and resistance zones.

Figure 11.8 Fibonacci moving average acting as a support

Figure 11.9 shows the FMA acting as a dynamic resistance zone during a bearish trend.

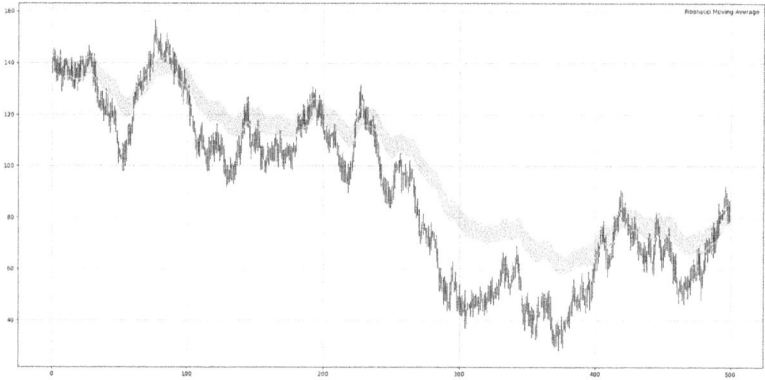

Figure 11.9 Fibonacci moving average acting as a resistance

The next chapter will equip you with the necessary skills to evaluate the performance of your strategies, but will also show you how to create a performance evaluation function that you can use to evaluate every indicator and strategy you have seen in the book.

CHAPTER 12

Performance Evaluation in Python

Performance evaluation is a critical aspect of trading that helps us assess how well strategies or portfolios are performing. Evaluating performance isn't just about looking at profits and losses; it involves a comprehensive analysis of various metrics that provide insights into risk, return, and overall strategy effectiveness. Additionally, performance evaluation helps in identifying the market conditions under which a strategy performs best and where it may struggle. This chapter will discuss some concepts of performance evaluation, as well as present a few back-testing cases.

Net Return

The most fundamental profitability indicator is the net return. It is calculated as follows:

$$\text{Net return} = \left(\frac{\text{Final balance}}{\text{Initial balance}} - 1 \right) \times 100$$

The net return serves as a normalizer when different amount of capital is used. Take the following examples:

- Portfolio A started the year with $1,000,000 and ended it with $1,100,000.
- Portfolio B started the year with $30,000 and ended it with $33,000.

The net profit from portfolio A was $100,000, and $3,000 from portfolio B. This represents a big gap in the amount of dollars made. However, the net return for both portfolios was 10%.

Hit Ratio

The hit ratio, also known as the win ratio or accuracy, is a key performance metric that indicates the percentage of trades that are profitable out of the total number of trades taken. It's a simple yet powerful tool used to assess the effectiveness of a trader's strategy. The hit ratio is calculated as the number of winning trades divided by the total number of trades:

$$\text{Hit ratio} = \left(\frac{\text{Number of winning trades}}{\text{Total number of trades}} \right) \times 100$$

For example, if a trader executes 100 trades and 60 of them make money, the hit ratio is 60%. A high hit ratio (e.g., above 50%) suggests that the majority of trades are winners. However, it doesn't guarantee profitability unless the gains from winning trades outweigh the losses from losing trades. A low hit ratio (e.g., 40% or below) indicates that fewer trades are profitable. Traders with a low hit ratio can still be profitable if the average gain on winning trades is significantly higher than the average loss on losing trades. This is where the risk-reward ratio enters.

Risk-Reward Ratio

The risk-reward ratio measures how much a trader stands to gain (or has gained) on average for every dollar risked. The formula is as follows:

$$\text{Risk} - \text{reward ratio} = \frac{\text{Average gain per profitable trade}}{\text{Average loss per unprofitable trade}}$$

A strategy with a lower hit ratio but a high risk-reward ratio can still be profitable. Conversely, a strategy with a high hit ratio but a poor risk-reward ratio might not be sustainable in the long run. Take a look at the following two examples:

- Trader A has a hit ratio of 80% with an average profit of $100 per winning trade and an average loss of $250 per losing trade. The risk-reward ratio is 0.40.
- Trader B has a hit ratio of 40% with an average profit of $300 per winning trade and an average loss of $100 per losing trade. The risk-reward ratio is 3.00.

Although Trader A wins more often, Trader B might be more profitable due to the higher reward compared to risk. A higher hit ratio can provide psychological comfort, as frequent wins can boost confidence. However, you must be cautious of overconfidence, which can lead to larger losses. A general rule of thumb in trading states that the risk-reward ratio must be at least around 1.50 to 2.00.

Expectancy

The expectancy metric is a way to evaluate the average amount you can expect to win or lose per trade over a series of trades. It gives insight into the profitability of a trading strategy by considering both the win rate and the average gain/loss ratio. Expectancy helps determine if a strategy has a positive or negative edge. The formula is as follows:

$$\text{Expectancy} = \left(\text{Hit ratio} \times \text{average gain}\right) - \left(\left[1 - \text{hit ratio}\right] \times \text{average loss}\right)$$

A positive expectancy means the strategy, on average, generates a profit over time. In contrast, a negative expectancy means the strategy will likely result in a loss over the course of time. Consider a trader with a 70% hit ratio, a $100 average gain per winning trade, and $400 average loss per losing trade. The expectancy is therefore:

$$Expectancy = (0.7 \times 100) - ((1 - 0.7) \times 400) = -50$$

Despite having a 70% hit ratio, the expectancy is $-\$50$ due to large losses from the losing trades.

Profit Factor

The ratio of total profits to total losses is known as the profit factor, and it is another measure of profitability. It makes sense that a strategy is lucrative if the profit factor is greater than 1.00 and less profitable if it is less than 1.00. The profit component is represented as follows:

$$\text{Profit factor} = \frac{\text{Total gains from trades}}{\left|\text{Total losses from trades}\right|}$$

Since it considers both the strategy's gains and losses rather than fo-
cusing on one side of the equation, the profit factor is a valuable metric
for assessing the profitability of a trading strategy. A trading strategy with
$54,012 in earnings and $29,988 in losses has a profit factor of 1.80.

Sharpe and Sortino Ratios

The Sharpe ratio measures the excess return per unit of total risk, where
risk is defined by the standard deviation of returns. It helps determine if
returns are due to smart investment decisions or excessive risk-taking. The
ratio is commonly used for comparing different strategies or assets on a
risk-adjusted basis. The formula is:

$$\text{Sharpe ratio} = \frac{x_p - r_f}{\sigma_p}$$

With x_p representing the average portfolio return, r_f representing the risk-
free rate on a government bond, and σ_p representing the standard deviation
of the portfolio's returns. A higher Sharpe ratio indicates a better risk-adjusted
return. A Sharpe ratio above 1 is considered good, above 2 is very good, and
above 3 is excellent. However, it can be skewed by high volatility in both
directions. The Sortino ratio is a variation of the Sharpe ratio but focuses only
on *downside* risk, which is more relevant since it captures only the negative
volatility or losses. This makes it particularly useful for strategies that seek to
limit losses rather than overall volatility. The formula is:

$$\text{Sortino ratio} = \frac{x_p - r_f}{\sigma_{dp}}$$

With x_p representing the average portfolio return, r_f representing the
risk-free rate on a government bond, and σ_{dp} representing the standard
deviation of the portfolio's negative returns. A higher Sortino ratio is preferable and indicates a higher return relative to the downside risk. Because
it ignores positive volatility, it's often more suitable for strategies that focus on reducing losses over general volatility.

Back-Testing Best Practices

Back-testing is a sensible tool to understand and hard to master. With
back-testing, the best you can hope for is that the future results can look

a little similar to the past results. There are some best practices to keep in mind in order to ensure a proper framework. First, ensure your historical data is accurate and free from gaps or errors. Incomplete or inaccurate data can lead to false results. Use the appropriate time frames (daily, intraday, and so on) depending on the strategy. For high-frequency strategies, minute or tick data is essential. You must also make sure to simulate realistic assumptions by incorporating reasonable trading fees, slippage, spreads, and commissions into your back-testing model. Ensure that the asset being traded is liquid enough for your strategy, especially for large positions or high-frequency strategies. Also, consider the time between signal generation and order execution. Perfect execution is rare in real markets. After back-testing, perform walk-forward testing to simulate how your strategy would perform in unseen data over time. This prevents overfitting to historical data. Be cautious of overoptimizing parameters to fit past data. Overfitting leads to great historical performance but poor real-world results (limit the number of parameters and focus on simple, robust strategies). Another important environment control system is to test your strategy in different market conditions (bullish, bearish, sideways) to assess its adaptability. You can also use different time periods for testing to ensure the strategy is not specific to a particular market environment. You can also compare the results of your strategy with a benchmark (e.g., S&P 500). Beating the benchmark consistently adds credibility. Test your strategy across a range of parameter values (e.g., moving average lengths, RSI thresholds). This shows how sensitive the performance is to small changes in parameter settings.

Evaluating a Simple Moving Average Cross Strategy

Let's back-test a known simple trading strategy, the moving average cross. The strategy is based on the crossover of two moving averages—typically a short-term and a long-term moving average. When these moving averages cross each other, it suggests a shift in market momentum, which traders use to make trading decisions. The trading signals are as follows:

- A bullish signal occurs when the short-term moving average crosses over the long-term moving average (referred to as a golden cross).

- A bearish signal occurs when the short-term moving average crosses under the long-term moving average (referred to as a death cross).

Before we start, let's make sure we understand the framework and expectations of this type of back-testing. The back-tests presented in this section and the following ones are intended purely for illustrative and educational purposes. They cover only a limited time period, are based on a small selection of assets, and do not account for the full investment universe. No attempt has been made to optimize performance—hyperparameters have been chosen arbitrarily, and transaction costs, slippage, and changing market regimes are not considered. As such, the results should neither be interpreted as indicative of real-world performance nor used to draw any investment conclusions. The goal of this exercise is to demonstrate the process of back-testing and to provide a framework for interpreting results when more rigorous, realistic testing is performed. Use the following code to create the logic of the strategy.

```
def moving_average_cross_strategy(my_time_series, short_moving_average=30, long_moving_average=50):
    my_time_series['bullish_signal'] = 0
    my_time_series['bearish_signal'] = 0
    my_time_series = moving_average(my_time_series, source='close', ma_lookback=short_moving_average, output_name='short_moving_average', ma_type='SMA')
    my_time_series = moving_average(my_time_series, source='close', ma_lookback=long_moving_average, output_name='long_moving_average', ma_type='SMA')
    for i in range(0, len(my_time_series)):
        # bullish signal
        if my_time_series['short_moving_average'].iloc[i] > my_time_series['long_moving_average'].iloc[i] and
        my_time_series['short_moving_average'].iloc[i-1] < my_time_series['long_moving_average'].iloc[i-1]:
            my_time_series.at[my_time_series.index[i+1], 'bullish_signal'] = 1
        # bearish signal
        elif my_time_series['short_moving_average'].iloc[i] < my_time_series['long_moving_average'].iloc[i]
            and my_time_series['short_moving_average'].iloc[i-1] >
            my_time_series['long_moving_average'].iloc[i-1]:
            my_time_series.at[my_time_series.index[i+1], 'bearish_signal'] = 1
    return my_time_series
```

The performance evaluation function can be found in the GitHub repository.[9] Figure 12.1 shows a signal chart showing the moving average cross strategy in action.

---

[9] GitHub link: https://github.com/sofienkaabar/mastering-financial-markets-in-python

Figure 12.1 **A moving average cross strategy**

The output of the strategy for the time period back-tested is as follows.

```
---Performance Evaluation---
Total hit ratio = 47.83 %
Bullish hit ratio = 56.52 %
Bearish hit ratio = 39.13 %
Profit factor = 0.96
Risk-reward ratio = 1.35
Expectancy = 0.96
Sharpe ratio = 0.87
Sortino ratio = 1.5
Number of bullish signals = 23
Number of bearish signals = 23
Number of signals = 46
```

Now, the aim is to analyze the strategy in detail, given the performance evaluation metrics. This strategy shows mixed performance. The overall hit ratio is 47.83%, with bullish trades performing better (56.52%) than bearish ones (39.13%), suggesting the strategy works better in rising markets. The profit factor (0.96) and expectancy (0.96) indicate it's not an interesting strategy, despite a decent risk-reward ratio (1.35)—wins are larger than losses, but not frequent enough to offset them. Risk-adjusted metrics are modest: the Sharpe ratio (0.87) is below the ideal threshold of 1, though the Sortino ratio (1.5) shows better downside protection. With 46 trades evenly split between long and short, the poor bearish performance suggests the need for filtering or biasing toward bullish setups. The key takeaway: a good win/loss ratio isn't enough—profitability depends on the balance between accuracy, risk control, and market context.

Comparing the Perfected and Unperfected TD Setup Pattern

Previously in Chapter 9, you have seen a timing pattern called the TD setup. You have also seen that it has two variations, a perfected setup and an unperfected setup. Here's a summary of the differences between the two:

- A perfected TD setup where the low of bars 8 or 9 in the setup sequence must be less than the lows of bars 6 and 7 in the case of a bullish setup. On the other hand, for the bearish setup to be perfected, the high of bars 8 or 9 in the setup sequence must be greater than the highs of bars 6 and 7.
- An unperfected TD setup where the conditions relating to bars 8 and 9 seen in the previous point are not taken into account.

This section will back-test both variations and will come up with a basic conclusion after analyzing the performance. You will simply do the exercise twice, where the first time you will set **perfected** to **False** and the second time you will set **perfected** to **True**. Figure 12.2 shows two signal charts, where the one on the left is the TD setup that includes all the signals, and the one on the right is the TD setup that only takes into account perfected signals.

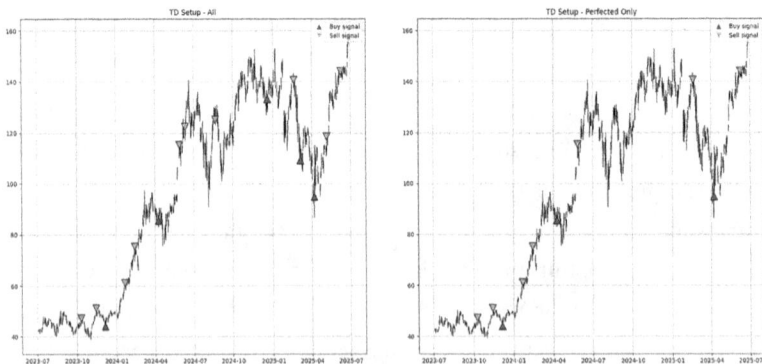

Figure 12.2 An unperfected TD strategy (left) *versus a perfected TD strategy* (right)

The unperfected setup has a higher hit ratio (47.22%) and more trades (72), but with a negative expectancy (−0.33) and low risk-reward ratio (0.95), it loses money despite frequent wins. The perfected setup, while less accurate (34.78% total hit rate), dramatically improves expectancy (1.41) and risk-reward ratio (3.07), meaning it wins less often but earns more when it does. Sharpe and Sortino ratios are slightly better in the perfected version, indicating improved downside risk control. In short, the perfected strategy trades less and wins less often, but with far more impact per trade—highlighting the value of quality signals over quantity. This back-test only considered a holding period of 10.

Evaluating a Simple Reversal Indicator

We'll take this opportunity to present a technical indicator that wasn't presented in previous chapters. We will define it, code it, and then back-test it. The Rob Booker reversal is an indicator composed of two classic indicators: the stochastic oscillator and the MACD. As you have already been exposed to the MACD, let's discuss the other indicator. The stochastic oscillator is a widely used momentum indicator that helps determine overbought or oversold conditions in a market. It compares a security's closing price to its price range over a specific period. It is based on the observation that as an asset's price rises, its closing price tends to be near the higher end of its price range, and when it falls, the closing price tends to be near the lower end. The formula is as follows.

$$\%K = \left(\frac{\text{Close price}_i - \text{lowest low}_n}{\text{Highest high}_n - \text{lowest low}_n} \right) \times 100$$
$$\%K \text{ smoothing} = \text{SMA}(\%K, n)$$
$$\%D = \text{SMA}(\%K \text{ smoothing}, n)$$

The oscillator is composed of two lines, %K smoothing and %D, with the latter being simply a 3-period SMA of %K smoothing. It's worth noting that %D is therefore a moving average applied to a moving average itself applied to the normalized values of the high, low, and close (HLC) data. Use the following code for the stochastic oscillator with the following parameters {14, 3, 3}, which are considered the default settings.

```
def stochastic_oscillator(my_time_series, k_lookback=14, k_smoothing_lookback=3, d_lookback=3):
    my_time_series['lowest_low']  = my_time_series['low'].rolling(window=k_lookback).min()
    my_time_series['highest_high'] = my_time_series['high'].rolling(window=k_lookback).max()
    my_time_series['%K'] = 100 * ((my_time_series['close'] - my_time_series['lowest_low']) / \
            (my_time_series['highest_high'] - my_time_series['lowest_low']))
    my_time_series['%K_smoothing'] =
                        my_time_series['%K'].rolling(window=k_smoothing_lookback).mean()
    my_time_series['%D'] = my_time_series['%K_smoothing'].rolling(window=d_lookback).mean()
    my_time_series = my_time_series.drop(columns=['lowest_low', 'highest_high'])
    return my_time_series.dropna()
```

Figure 12.3 shows EURUSD with its stochastic oscillator{14, 3, 3}. Notice how it's bounded between 0 and 100, with values close to 30 representing oversold conditions and values close to 70 representing overbought conditions.

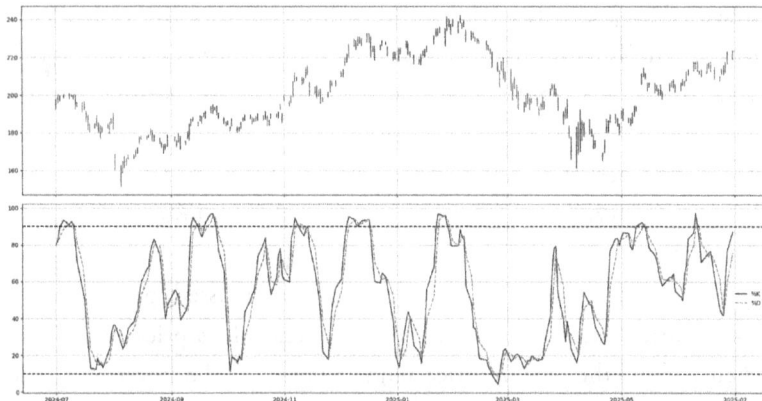

Figure 12.3 Stochastic oscillator

The Rob Booker reversal indicator combines the stochastic oscillator with the MACD in the following manner:

- A bullish signal is generated whenever the MACD line crosses over the zero line. Also, the %K smoothing of the stochastic oscillator (70, 10, 10) must be below 30.
- A bearish signal is generated whenever the MACD line crosses below the zero line. Also, the %K smoothing of the stochastic oscillator (70, 10, 10) must be above 70.

In other words, the indicator relies on a moving average cross while keeping potential on the stochastic oscillator to confirm the move. Use the following code to create a function that calculates the Rob Booker reversal indicator given an OHLC data frame.

Figure 12.4 shows the indicator in action.

Figure 12.4 Rob Booker's reversal indicator

Use the following code to calculate Rob Booker's reversal indicator.

```
def rob_booker_reversal(my_time_series):
  my_time_series = stochastic_oscillator(my_time_series, k_lookback=70, k_smoothing_lookback=10, d_lookback=10)
  my_time_series = macd(my_time_series, source='close')
  my_time_series['bullish_signal'] = 0
  my_time_series['bearish_signal'] = 0
  for i in range(0, len(my_time_series)):
    # bullish signal
    if my_time_series['MACD_line'].iloc[i] > 0 and my_time_series['MACD_line'].iloc[i-1] < 0 and \
      my_time_series['%K_smoothing'].iloc[i] < 30:
      my_time_series.at[my_time_series.index[i+1], 'bullish_signal'] = 1
    # bearish signal
    elif my_time_series['MACD_line'].iloc[i] < 0 and my_time_series['MACD_line'].iloc[i-1] > 0 and \
      my_time_series['%K_smoothing'].iloc[i] > 70:
      my_time_series.at[my_time_series.index[i+1], 'bearish_signal'] = 1
  return my_time_series
```

Applying the performance evaluation function gives the following results.

```
---Performance Evaluation---
Total hit ratio = 60.0 %
Bullish hit ratio = 60.0 %
```

Bearish hit ratio = 60.0 %
Profit factor = 1.5
Risk-reward ratio = 2.57
Expectancy = 4.18
Sharpe ratio = 0.86
Sortino ratio = 2.05
Number of bullish signals = 5
Number of bearish signals = 10
Number of signals = 15

It seems that this strategy shows a strong and balanced performance across both long and short trades, with a 60% hit ratio for each. Though the sample size is small (15 total trades), the metrics are promising. A profit factor of 1.5 and a high risk-reward ratio of 2.57 suggest that profits outweigh losses both in frequency and magnitude. The expectancy of 4.18 indicates significant average gains per trade. Risk-adjusted returns are solid, with a Sortino ratio of 2.05, reflecting good control over downside volatility.

Conclusion

In this book, we embarked on a comprehensive journey through the landscape of modern technical analysis, leveraging Python as a powerful tool to uncover actionable insights in financial markets. We explored a wide range of technical analysis techniques, from classic indicators to advanced modern indicators and patterns, demonstrating how Python can enhance and streamline the analytical process. By adding code snippets, charts, and detailed explanations, I aimed to empower readers with both the theoretical understanding and practical skills needed. Throughout the chapters, we saw how Python's versatility and robust libraries offer an accessible yet powerful platform for implementing technical analysis. Whether it was calculating moving averages, plotting candlestick charts, or back-testing trading strategies, Python allowed us to move from theory to practice with ease. We also delved into the intricacies of momentum indicators, trend analysis, and volume-based charting tools, showing how these traditional methods can be revitalized with modern technology and modern hypotheses. The automation of these processes not only saves time but also allows for more rigorous and systematic analysis, reducing the potential for human error. One of the key takeaways from this book is the importance of combining multiple indicators and approaches to form a holistic view of the market. No single indicator is foolproof; the true power of technical analysis lies in its ability to synthesize various signals into a coherent strategy. The use of data-driven decision making, reinforced by Python's capabilities, enables a more objective approach to trading, which is crucial in a market environment often driven by emotion and speculation. In conclusion, the intersection of technical analysis and Python represents a powerful synergy, offering both depth and breadth in financial market analysis. This book has aimed to provide not only a toolkit of modern techniques but also the inspiration to continue exploring and innovating. The financial markets are constantly evolving, and with them, the tools and methods we use must also evolve.